I0017531

macOS Sonoma
USER GUIDE

The Complete Manual for Your Mac Systems for Beginners and Seniors with Tips, Tricks, and Pictorial Illustrations

Ron Oscar

All rights reserved

Copyright © 2023.Ron Oscar

No part of this manual may be reproduced, stored in a retrieval system, or transmitted and used by any means without the permission of the writer or publisher.

TABLE OF CONTENTS
CHAPTER ONE

CHAPTER TWO

CHAPTER THREE

CHAPTER SEVEN

CHAPTER EIGHT

CHAPTER ONE

BEGIN WITH MAC DESKTOP FEATURES

MENU BAR

On your Mac, the menu bar extends along the top of the display. Utilize the menus and icons located in the menu bar to select commands, execute tasks, and verify the current status.

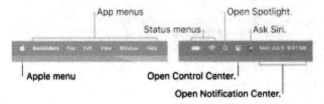

The navigation bar is present. The application and Apple menus are located on the left. Notification Centre, Spotlight, Control Centre, and Siri are located on the right.

It is possible to configure an option that will conceal the menu bar automatically when the user moves the cursor to the top of the screen.

The Apple Menu

The Apple menu, situated in the upper-left corner of the display, comprises shortcut keys for frequently used actions, including app updates, System Settings access, screen lock, and Mac shutdown.

Applications Interfaces

The location of app menus are adjacent the Apple menu. The application's name is displayed in italics, followed by additional menus, which are frequently labeled with common designations like *File, Edit, Format, or Window*. The Help menu of each application facilitates access to information regarding the application's use.

Much of the commands in each menu are accessible in the majority of applications. Open, for instance, is frequently accessible via the File menu. To learn more about the symbols utilized in the menu command keyboard shortcuts.

Status Menus
Typically portrayed as symbols, the items (sometimes referred to as status menus) located at the far right of the menu bar allow you to customize functions (like the keyboard luminance) or check the battery charge status of your Mac.

To display additional options or information, select a status menu symbol. To display a list of the accessible networks, for instance, select Wi-Fi; to enable or disable Dark Mode or Night Shift, select Display. Selecting which items to display in the menu pane is possible.

In order to reconfigure status menus, drag an icon while holding down the Command key. To expeditiously eliminate a status menu, hold down the Command key while dragging the menu icon from the menu bar.

The Spotlight
Clicking the Spotlight symbol in the menu area will allow you to conduct web and Mac-based searches for specific items. Refer to Search using Spotlight.

Control Center
By selecting the Control Centre icon, one can access Control Centre, which contains frequently used applications including AirDrop, AirPlay, Focus, as well as others.

Siri
Select the Siri icon that appears in your menu bar to use Siri to perform actions such as opening files or applications, conducting web searches, or opening files or applications on your Mac.

The Notification Center
Select the time and date at the end of the navigation bar to access the Notification Centre, from where you may catch up on missed alerts and examine appointments, notes, weather, as well as more.

DESKTOP

The Dock appears at the bottom of the screen, while the menu bar appears at the top. Between them is an area known as the desktop. Working on the desktop is the primary activity.

A Mac desktop configured for a dark appearance, featuring a dark program window, Dock, and menu bar.

Modify The Desktop Image

You have the option of selecting a dynamic desktop image that changes automatically throughout the day or uploading one of your own.

Personalize The Desktop's Appearance

You have the option to give the menu bar, desktop image, Dock, and in-built applications a pale or dark appearance.

Implement Desktop Notifications

Notifications regarding inbound emails or messages, impending events, and more are displayed in the upper-right corner of the desktop. From the notification, you can request a reminder, respond to a message, and perform additional actions. How and timing of notifications are customizable. Enable a Focus to halt them when you need to put your mind on a specific task.

File Organization on the Desktop

Stacks allow you to organize files by type or other criteria together on one side of the desktop, which is convenient if you prefer to have files readily available. Whenever you add a document to the desktop, it is inserted into a stack.

Locate a Window within the Desktop

You may utilize Mission Control to move open windows from the desktop so that you can access it, or to display a basic view of all the stuff that is open on the desktop, making it easy to locate the desired window.

Implement Several Desktops

Additional desktop spaces can be created in order to organize duties on particular desktops. For instance, one could effortlessly transition between the two while concentrating on a project on another desktop while managing email on the former. Additionally, you can personalize each interface to correspond with the task at hand.

SPOTLIGHT

Spotlight enables you to locate documents, emails, applications, and many more items on your Mac with ease. You can also obtain news, sports scores, conditions for the weather, stock prices, and many more via Siri Suggestions. Additionally, Spotlight can convert and conduct calculations for you.

Say to Siri, "How many centimeters are there in an inch?" or "Explain the term "parboil.""

Try To Locate Something
- Perform one or more of the following actions on your Mac:
  - ✓ If displayed, select the Spotlight symbol from the menu bar.
  - ✓ Utilize the Command-Space tab.
  - ✓ When accessible, select the function key row on the computer's keyboard.

The Spotlight window can be dragged to any location on the desktop.

Add the Spotlight symbol to the menu bar via the Control Centre settings if it is not already present.

- Enter the desired information into the search field; results will appear when you type.

When Spotlight displays the best matches, select one to launch or preview it. Additionally, variants of your search are suggested by Spotlight and might show up in Spotlight or on the internet.

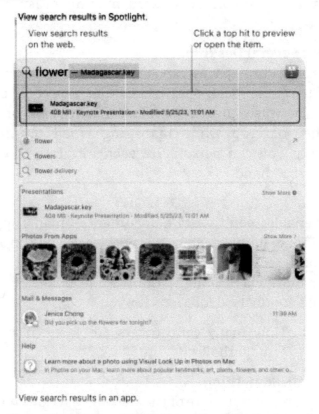

The Spotlight window displays the results of searches beneath the search field at the highest point of the screen.

- In the outcomes, perform one of the subsequent actions:
- ✓ View the outcomes of a recommended search in Spotlight: Tap the item that is highlighted by the Spotlight icon.
- ✓ View the results of a recommended web search: Select an item that is denoted by an arrow symbol.
- ✓ Explode an item: It requires a double-tap. Enter the item's name followed by the Return key press.

This operation may launch an application, including Messages, Help Viewer ⑦, and others.

- ✓ To activate or deactivate a setting, including VoiceOver, select the corresponding option via a click while searching in Spotlight.
- ✓ Perform a rapid action: You might be able to perform a rapid action when you enter a phone number, email address, date, or time, including initiating a FaceTime call or composing an email.
- ✓ Display the file's location on your Mac: After selecting the desired file, hold down the Command key. The location of the file is displayed at the bottom of the preview window.
- ✓ Copies of items: A file can be dragged to the taskbar or a Finder window.
- ✓ View every outcome in the Finder from your Mac: After locating the search results at the bottom, select Search in Finder.

When an application reaches its designated time limit in the Screen Time settings or during periods of inactivity, the app icons displayed in the results become dimmed and replaced the icon with an hourglass icon.

Use Spotlight To Perform Conversions And Calculations

In the Spotlight search field, you can input a mathematical expression, currency quantity, temperature, or anything else to obtain an instant conversion or calculation.

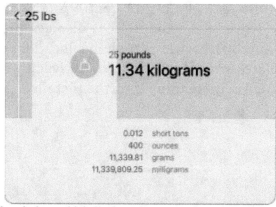

The Spotlight window, which displays the conversion results below, and enter a weight for entering in the search box at the highest point of the window.

- **The calculations involve** the input of a mathematical expression, including 2020/15 or 956*23.94.
- **The process of converting currencies**: Include a monetary value in the currency field, such as "300 krone in euros" or "100 yen."
- **Conversions of temperatures:** Input a temperature, such as "340K in F" "98.8F" or "32C."
- **Conversion of measurements:** Input a unit of measurement, such as "32 feet to meters," "25 pounds," or "54 yards to 23 stones."
- For conversions to world clocks, enter a phrase describing the local time in a particular location, such as "time in Paris" or "Japan local time."

CONTROL CENTRE

Control Centre provides fast access to important macOS configurations, including AirDrop, Wi-Fi, and Focus. It is possible to modify the Control Centre by including additional information, such as battery status, accessibility shortcuts, or quick user toggling.

A green dot denotes an active camera; an orange dot adjacent to the Control Centre icon in the menu bar signifies the active microphone; and an arrow indicates the active location on your Mac. When both the camera and microphone are active, only a green dot is visible. The Control Centre interface may include a field at the top of the window that displays the applications that are utilizing the user's microphone, location, or camera. By selecting the aforementioned field, the Privacy window will be displayed, potentially containing further details.

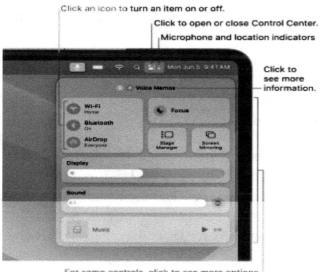

Click an icon to turn an item on or off.

Click to open or close Control Center.

Microphone and location indicators

Click to see more information.

For some controls, click to see more options.
For Stage Manger, click to turn it on or off.

Control Centre is located in the upper-right corner of the display and includes, among other things, buttons for Wi-Fi, Focus, Sound, as well as Now Playing.

Implement The Control Centre

- Select Control Centre from the menu bar on your Mac.
- Perform any one of the following tasks with Control Centre items:

✓ To increase or decrease a setting, drag a slider; for instance, to modify the volume on your Mac, drag the Sound slider.

✓ Select an icon to enable or disable a feature; for instance, to enable Bluetooth® or AirDrop.

✓ Press an item (or its arrow) to display additional options; for instance, to display your Focus list and toggle a focus on or off, select Screen Mirroring to select a target display, or click Focus to display your Focus list.

If you utilize a particular item frequently, you can transfer it from the Control Centre to the menu bar to keep it accessible. In order to eliminate an item compared to the menu bar, simultaneously drag the item while holding down the Command key.

Modify the Control Centre

- Select Apple > System Preferences on your Mac, then select

Control Centre in the sidebar. (Depth may require the user to navigate.)

- In the categories on the right, select configurations for the products.

✓ **Modules of the Control Centre:** The items within this section remain visible in the Control Centre at all times and cannot be removed. You have the option to display them within the menu bar as well. To select an option, select the pop-up menu adjacent to the item in question.

✓ **Additional Modules:** The contents of this section may be added to the Control Centre or the menu bar. Turn on or off each option beneath an item. There may be additional parameters available for certain products.

✓ **Menu Bar Only:** In addition to selecting options for the menu bar clock, you can also add other items to the menu bar, including Spotlight, Siri, Time Machine, as well as VPN status.

SIRI

Siri can be utilized on a Mac to perform routine activities such as scheduling a meeting, launching an application, and obtaining instant responses to inquiries.

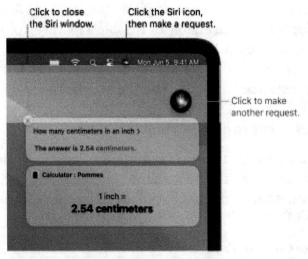

The region in the upper-right corner of the Mac desktop that contains the Siri window contains the query "How many centimeters are there in an inch?" and the corresponding answer (which is the transformation from Calculator). Submit an additional request by clicking the symbol in the upper-right corner of the Siri interface. By selecting the close option, the Siri window can be closed.

Activate Siri

- Select Apple > System Preferences on your Mac, and then select Siri & Spotlight in the sidebar. (Depth may require the user to navigate.)
- If Not Already Enabled, toggle Ask Siri to the right and then select Enable.

When you attempt to activate Siri without selecting the option, you are prompted to do so. Siri functionality requires an active internet connection.

- When asked how Siri and Dictation could be improved, select either of the following options:
- ✓ Disseminate audio recordings: Permit Apple to save the audio of your Mac's Siri as well as Dictation interactions by selecting Share Audio Recordings. Apple may examine a preserved audio sample.
- ✓ Avoid disclosing audio recordings: Select "Not Now."

Should you subsequently decide to share or discontinue sharing audio recordings, navigate to Apple > System Preferences > Privacy & Security in the sidebar. (Depth may require the user to navigate.) Select Analytics & Improvements from the menu on the right, then toggle the Improve Siri & Dictation choice on or off. Refer to Modify security and privacy settings.

It is possible to remove audio interactions at any time; they have been linked with a random identifier as well as are older than six months; for more information, refer to the Delete Siri as well as the Dictation history section.

- Perform one of the following:
- ✓ **Employ "Hey Siri" or "Siri":** To initiate the use of Siri, activate the "Listen for" feature or select the desired phrase, if applicable to your device and language. By activating

"Allow Siri when locked" in conjunction with this option, it is possible to utilize Siri while your Mac has been locked or in slumber mode.

To determine whether "Siri" or "Hey Siri" is compatible with the gadget as well as language.

✓ **Configure a keyboard shortcut:** From the "Keyboard shortcut" pop-up menu, select or construct your shortcut to activate Siri.

Tip: To activate Siri, select and hold the Microphone key if it is present in the series of function keys, or employ the keyboard's shortcut.

✓ **Select the way Siri speaks:** Select a language via the Language pop-up menu that appears. Select the desired voice for Siri from the Voice Variety as well as Siri Voice options after clicking Select next to "Siri voice" to observe a preview. (Some languages might offer a single option.)

✓ **To silence Siri**, Select Siri Responses and deactivate "Voice feedback"; the Siri response will remain in the window but will not be spoken.

✓ **Display the words of Siri on-screen:** To enable "Always display Siri captions," select Siri Responses and then toggle "Always show captions."

Display your words on-screen: Select Siri Responses, then toggle "Show speech at all times" on.

Select Siri Suggestions and Privacy, then About Siri and Privacy.

Choose Apple > System Settings, then select Control Centre in the sidebar, to add Siri to the menu bar. (Depth may require the user to navigate.) Select Show in Menu Bar adjacent to Siri by navigating to Menu Bar Only on the right.

Enable Siri

Siri functionality is contingent upon an active internet connection.

- To enable Siri on your Mac, perform one of the subsequent:
  ✓ If the Microphone key is present in the series of function keys, press and hold it; otherwise, utilize the keyboard shortcut specified in the Siri & Spotlight settings.
  ✓ Select Siri from the menu. Using the Control Centre settings, you can add it if it is not currently displayed.
  ✓ Select Siri using the Touch Bar on your Mac, if one is present.
  ✓ Pronounce "Siri" or "Hey Siri" (if enabled and accessible via the Siri & Spotlight settings).
- Propose a request, such as "Arrange a meeting for 9:00" or "Remember the outcome of the game from last night."

With Location Services enabled, the moment you submit a request, the precise whereabouts of your device will be ascertained. This setting can be modified via System Preferences > Permit applications to detect the precise spot of your Mac.

Disable Siri

- Select Apple > System Preferences on your Mac, and then select Siri & Spotlight in the sidebar. (Depth may require the user to navigate.)
- At the right, deactivate Ask Siri.

NOTIFICATION CENTRE

By accessing Notification Centre on your Mac, you can utilize elements to view schedules, birthdays, weather conditions, top headlines, and other information directly from the desktop. Additionally, you can catch up on ignored notifications.

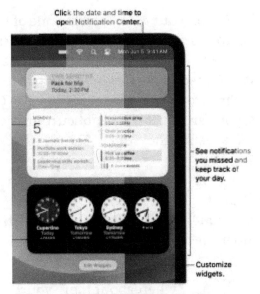

Notification Centre widgets and notifications.

Launch Or Dismiss The Notification Centre

Perform any one of the following on the Mac:

- **Launch the Notification Centre**: Utilize the menu bar to access the time and date, or use two fingers to move it left from the right margin of the trackpad.
- To dismiss the notification center, select the date and time from the menu bar, select anywhere across the desktop, or slide right with two fingertips toward the right margin of the touchpad.

Utilize Notification Centre Notifications On Your Mac

While hovering the pointer over a notification in the Notification Centre, perform one of the subsequent actions:

- **Expand or collapse a stack of alerts:** When the notifications of an application are grouped, a stack of multiple notifications is created. To display every notification in the stack, expand the stack by clicking anywhere in the upper notification. To hide the stack entirely, select "Show less."
- **Engage in action:** Select the action by clicking it. For

instance, in a notification from the Mail application, select Reply; in a notification from the Calendar application, select Snooze.

Click the arrow next to an action to access additional alternatives. To respond to a phone call employing the Messages application, for instance, select Reply with Message by clicking the arrow next to Decline.

- **View further details:** Tap the alert to launch the item within the application. To display additional information in the notification, click the arrow that appears to the right of the application name.
- Modify the notification settings of an application by selecting the More button that appears when an arrow icon appears to the right of the application's name. From there, select the desired action, such as muting or disabling notifications, or by accessing the Notifications settings menu.
- Eliminate a specific notification or an entire collection of notifications: Select Clear or Clear All from the menu.

Utilize Widgets In The Mac Notification Centre
Perform the following within the Notification Centre:

- **View further details**: By clicking on any element within a widget, the corresponding settings, application, or webpage can be accessed. To illustrate, by selecting a widget such as the Weather widget to launch a web browser as well as view the complete forecast, or the Reminders widget to access the Reminders app, one can navigate to the Date & Time preferences.
- **To adjust the size of a widget**: Control-click a widget, then select alternative dimensions.
- **To delete a widget**, hover the cursor over it while holding down the Option key, and then select the Remove icon.

You can modify and personalize the elements that are displayed in the Notification Centre.

Recommendation: Employ a Focus setting, such as Work or Do Not Disturb, to restrict the visibility of notifications or eliminate interruptions.

THE DOCK

Utilizing the Dock on the Mac desktop grants users convenient access to frequently utilized applications and functions, such as the Launchpad as well as the Trash.

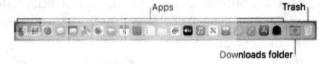

The Dock, contains application icons, the Downloads heap, and the Trash.

It is possible to add a folder for items downloaded from the internet and up to three recently utilized applications that are not already in the Dock. The Dock is situated along the bottom border of the display by default; however, an alternative location along either the right or left edges can be specified via an option.

Item Access In The Dock

While in the Dock on the computer, perform one of the subsequent:

- To launch an application, tap its icon. To launch the Finder, for instance, select the Finder icon from the Dock.
- **To access a file in an application**: Simply hover the file over the icon of the application. To launch a document that was created in Pages, for instance, drag the file over the Pages symbol in the Dock.
- **Display a particular item within the Finder**: Command-click the icon of the item.
- **Initiate the previous application while hiding the current one**: Option-click the icon of the current application.
- **Change to a different application and disable all others**: Press and hold Option-Command-click the application's

icon to transition to it.

Perform Additional Operations On Items Within The Dock

While using the Dock on the computer, perform one of the subsequent:

- **Present a menu of shortcuts for actions**: To display the auxiliary menu of an item, perform a control-click. From there, select an action, including Show Recents, or click on a filename to initiate the file.
- **Force an application to terminate**: Control-click the application's icon and select Force Quit if it ceases to respond; however, unsaved modifications may be lost.

Rearrange, Add, Or Remove Dock Items

Perform one or more of the following actions on your Mac:

- **Insert a file into the Dock**: applications can be dragged to the left of the boundary that divides the recently used applications, or higher. Files and folders can be dragged to the right of the line that divides recently used applications, or below it. The asset is assigned an alias within the Dock.

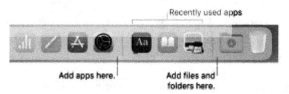

The terminus of the Dock displays the separator lines that appear
before and after the section for recently used applications.

When a folder is dragged to the Dock, it becomes visible as a layer. The Dock includes a Downloads folder by default.

- To unload an item from the Dock, simply drag the thing in question out of the port till the Remove button appears. On your Mac, only an alias has been deleted; the actual item remains.

Restoring the icon of an application from the Dock is a straightforward process, even if the app remains installed on your Mac. Reactivate the application to restore its icon in the Dock. Control-click the icon of the application, then select Options > Keep in Dock.

- To rearrange Dock items, simply drag an item to its new location.

A Handoff icon for the application running on your iPhone, iPad, iPod touch, or Apple Watch will appear in the Dock's upper-right corner.

Personalize The Dock

- Select Apple > System Preferences on your Mac, followed by Desktop & Dock in the sidebar. (Depth may require the user to navigate.)
- In the section to the right of Dock, modify the desired options.

For instance, you can modify the appearance of items in the Dock, reposition it along the screen's left or right boundary, or even conceal it.

Move the cursor over the boundary line in the Dock till a double arrow shows up, then click and drag the cursor down or up to rapidly modify the Dock's size. Control-clicking the separator will bring up a menu of additional shortcut actions.

Keyboard shortcuts can be employed to access the Dock. Fn-Control-F3 will transport you to the Dock. Press and hold both the Right and Left Arrow keys to navigate between icons. By pressing Return, an item can be opened.

A red badge on a Dock icon signifies that several actions are required in a particular application or system setting. A red emblem on the Mail symbol in the Dock, for instance, signifies that you have new messages to peruse.

FILE ORGANIZATION USING THE FINDER

Utilizing the Finder as the foundation of your Mac. A Finder window can be opened by clicking the Finder icon in the Dock, which resembles a blue smiley face.

The Dock's left side, with the Finder symbol located at its far left.

Finder windows are utilized to organize and gain access to virtually everything on a Mac.

A Finder window featuring a left-hand Finder sidebar. Four icons for modifying the way items are displayed in the window as well as more buttons for arranging and distributing items are located at the highest point of the window.

Observe YOUR STUFFS

Sidebar elements in the Finder can be selected to display files, applications, downloads, and more. Customize the sidebar to increase its utility. To increase the utility of the Finder window, enable the Preview pane.

Gain access to everything, anyplace

Utilize iCloud Drive for iCloud-based file and folder storage. They are accessible from any device to which the same Apple ID is applied.

Utilize Categories Or Folders To Organize

You may organize the files in folders if that is your preference. In iCloud Drive, in your Docs folder, or on your desktop, you may create new folders.

Additionally, files and folders can be annotated with relevant keywords to facilitate their retrieval.

Settle An Untidy Display

Stacks facilitate the organization of files into orderly desktop groups. Stacks may be categorized by type, date, or keywords. When you group by type, for instance, all of your images are placed in one layer and your presentations in another. Any newly added files are promptly stacked in the appropriate location, assisting in the automatic maintenance of order.

Select Your View

You can customize how objects appear in Finder windows. For instance, you are not limited to viewing your items in a list; gallery view enables you to visually navigate through your files as well as folders.

Transfer Folders Or Data

Using the Finder, you can duplicate a file or folder and send it to a nearby Mac, iPhone, or iPad. To initiate AirDrop, select the link in the sidebar. Refer to Utilize AirDrop to transfer files to nearby devices.

Alternatively, you can utilize the Touch Bar or select the Share icon from the Finder to transmit a file or folder via Mail, AirDrop, Messages, as well as other services. If the Share icon is not visible, select the More Toolbar Items link located at the end of the toolbar.

Distribute Folders Or Data

You can collaborate with other iCloud users on a file or folder stored in iCloud Drive. To begin, in the Finder, select a file or folder, click the Share icon (or utilize the Touch Bar), and then select Share File or Share Folder. If the Share icon is not visible, select the More Toolbar Items link located at the very end of the toolbar. Refer to Utilize iCloud for file and folder collaboration and sharing.

To view all of your iCloud Drive-stored documents, select the corresponding folder from the sidebar. Select the Shared folder to view only the papers that you're currently sharing, that have been shared with you, and on which you have been extended an invitation to collaborate. To modify the sidebar's contents, navigate to Finder > Settings.

Sync Data Among Your Mac As Well As Other Gadgets

By linking your iPhone, iPad, or iPod touch to your Mac, it is possible to transfer as well as update data between the two gadgets.

When a movie is added to a Mac, for instance, it can be synchronized with an iPhone so that it can be viewed on both gadgets.

Syncable items consist of movies, novels, podcasts, and music, among others.

Utilize Keyboard Shortcuts To Complete Tasks Rapidly

By employing keyboard shortcuts, one can efficiently execute routine operations.

CHAPTER TWO

THE INTERNET

ACCESSING THE INTERNET

Your Mac is capable of establishing an internet connection, regardless of location (home, work, or travel). Utilizing a Wi-Fi (wireless) or Ethernet (wired) link is a frequent practice. If neither option is accessible, an Instant Hotspot might suffice.

Apply Wi-Fi

The presence of an available Wi-Fi network is indicated by the Wi-Fi icon in the menu bar located at the highest point of the display. After selecting the icon, select a network to join. When a lock icon appears adjacent to the network name, it indicates that the network is password protected; in order to access that Wi-Fi network, you must input the password. Instructions for connecting via Wi-Fi.

Employ Ethernet

Ethernet connectivity is available via Ethernet networks, DSL, and cable modems. Connect a cable with Ethernet to the receptacle denoted by the icon on your Mac, assuming Ethernet is operational. You may utilize an adapter to link the Ethernet cable with the USB or Thunderbolt interface on your computer if your Mac lacks an Ethernet port by default. Guidelines for configuring Ethernet.

Implement An Instant Hotspot

In the absence of a Wi-Fi or Ethernet link, it is possible that you can establish an internet connection via the personal hotspot on the iPad or iPhone using your Mac as well as Instant Hotspot. Connecting via an iOS device (iPhone or iPad).

On the go, at home, or in the office

Your Internet service provider may provide Wi-Fi or Ethernet connections for use at home. Confer with your Internet service provider if you are uncertain about the nature of the access you possess.

You may have access to a Wi-Fi or Ethernet internet connection while at work.

You can utilize Wi-Fi nodes (public wireless networks) or Instant Hotspot on the computer while on the move, provided that your Mac as well as phone provider support it. Bear in mind that in order to utilize certain Wi-Fi locations, you may be required to pay a fee, provide a password, or consent to the terms of service.

EDIT AS WELL AS VIEW DOCUMENTS ON A MAC USING QUICK LOOK

Quick Look provides a rapid, full-screen glimpse of virtually any file type without requiring the user to access the file. Utilize Markup, rotate images, as well as trim audio and video recordings all from within the Quick Look window.

An image accompanied by icons to annotate, rotate, share, or launch the Preview application within the Quick Look window.

Utilize Quick Look to locate items in various locations, including Finder windows, the desktop, emails, as well as messages.

- Choose any number of items on your Mac, then click the

Space bar.

Opens the Quick Look window. When multiple objects are selected, the most recently selected item is displayed initially.

- Perform the following within the Quick Look window:
  - ✓ To resize the window, manipulate its corners with your mouse. Select the Full-Screen icon located in the Quick Look window's upper-left corner. To dismiss a full screen, select the dismiss Full-Screen button that appears after dragging the pointer to the bottom of the window.
  - ✓ To adjust the size of an item, utilize the Command-Plus (+) key to enlarge the image, and the Command-Minus (−) key to reduce it.
  - ✓ To rotate an object, hold down the Option key while clicking the Rotate Right button or press down on the Rotate Left button. To continue rotating the item, click again.
  - ✓ To annotate an item, select Markup from the menu.
  - ✓ To crop a video or audio segment, select Trim▸☐◂ from the menu, and then drag the yellow handles within the trimming bar. To preview your modifications, press Play. To begin again, select Revert. Click the "Done" button when you are ready to save your modifications, and then select whether to replace the existing file or generate a new one.
  - ✓ To navigate through selected items (if multiple items are present), click the Left Arrow or Right Arrow key or use the arrows located in the upper-left corner of the window. Select the Play icon in full-screen mode to observe each item as a slideshow.
  - ✓ To display the items in a grid (if multiple items were selected), select Command-Return or select the Index Sheet icon.
  - ✓ To launch a file, select Open with [App].
  - ✓ To share an item, select the desired method after clicking the Share icon.

✓ If the item is a photograph or screenshot, it is possible to separate the subject from the background to copy it. Click and hold the image, then select Copy Subject. The subject can now be copied and pasted into a note, email, document, or text message.

• Press the dismiss button or the Space bar when you are finished to dismiss the Quick Look window.

When a Live Photo is opened in the Quick Look window, an automatic video portion of the image is played. To re-enable the image, select Live Photo from the menu in the lower-left corner.

SCREEN CAPTURES OR SCREEN RECORDINGS

Screenshots and recordings of the display are both possible on a Mac via keyboard shortcuts or the Screenshot application. Screenshot offers a panel of tools that facilitate the capture of screenshots as well as screen recordings, with choices to control the captured content, such as including the pointer or actions or setting a timer delay.

Display Images And Screencasts By Utilizing Screenshot

• Select Shift-Command-5 (or utilize Launchpad) on your computer to launch the Screenshot as well as display the tools.

The panel for screenshots.

• To choose an appropriate instrument for selecting or recording content, either click on it or utilize the Touch Bar.

By dragging the frame or its boundaries, you can reposition a portion of the screen or modify the dimensions of the area you intend to record or capture.

Action	Tool
Screen capture in its entirely	▭

Capture a window	
Capture a portion of the display	
Record the complete screen	
Record a portion of the display	

- Select the Options menu option.

The options that are accessible are distinct when distinguishing between screen recording and screenshotting. You may, for instance, specify the location of the file to be saved, enable the display of the mouse pointer or touches, or configure a timed delay.

A few seconds after being saved to the location you specify, the Show Floating Thumbnail option enables you to work more efficiently with a completed shot or recording. During this time, the thumbnail floats in the lower-right corner of the screen, allowing you to transfer the image into a document, annotate it, or distribute it.

- Commence the screen capture or screen recording:
  ✓ To capture a portion or the entire display, select Capture.
  ✓ To access a window, navigate to it with the mouse and then click on it.
  ✓ To make a recording, select Record. To halt the recording process, select Stop Recording from the menu bar.

While the Show Floating Thumbnail option is enabled, the following actions are available in the bottom-right corner of the display whilst the thumbnail is temporarily displayed:

  ✓ Right-click to save the file immediately and delete it.
  ✓ In a Finder window, document, email, or note, drag the thumbnail.
  ✓ A window will appear when you click the thumbnail, allowing you to annotate the screenshot, minimize the

recording, or distribute it.

An application may launch, contingent upon the location where the screenshot or recording was saved.

Capture Images By Utilizing Keyboard Shortcuts

A variety of keyboard shortcuts are available for capturing screenshots on a Mac. The desktop is where the files are stored.

To replicate a screenshot for pasting into another application or device, hold down the Control key while pressing and holding the other keys. To replicate the entire screen, for instance, enter Shift-Command-Control-3.

ACTION	SHORTCUT
Entirely capture the screen.	Press Shift- command 3.
Capture a portion of the display	After pressing Shift-Command-4, position the crosshair cursor to the desired starting point of the screenshot. When the desired area to be captured is visible, remove the mouse or touchpad icon after dragging it.
Capture the navigation bar or a window	After holding down Shift-Command-4, click the Space bar. To highlight a window or menu bar, hover the camera pointer over it and then click.
Capture Menu and menu object.	To capture menu items, launch the menu, select Shift-Command-4, and afterward drag the pointer across the desired items.
Display Screenshot	Hold the Shift-Command 5.
Capture the Touch Bar	Click Shift-Command-6.

These shortcuts are modifiable through the Keyboard preferences menu. Select Apple > System Settings on your Mac, then select

Keyboard in the sidebar, followed by Keyboard Shortcuts on the right, and finally Screenshots. (Depth may require the user to navigate.)

Screen recordings are stored as.mov files, while screenshots are preserved as.png files. Include the time and the words "Screenshot" or "Screen Recording" at the beginning of the filename.

The ability to capture images of windows may be limited in certain applications, including DVD Player.

ADJUSTING THE DISPLAY'S BRIGHTNESS

The luminance of the display can be modified either manually or automatically.

Utilize The Function Keys For Luminance

If the screen appears excessively brilliant or black, the luminance of your display can be adjusted.

- Simply select the corresponding brightness key or utilize the Control Strip on your Mac to adjust the brightness level.

Automated Luminance Adjustment

- To access the Displays option in the sidebar of an Apple menu > System Preferences, select Ambient Light Sensor. (Depth may require the user to navigate.)
- Select "Automatically adjust brightness" from the menu on the right.

You can manually modify the brightness if the "Automatically adjust brightness" option is not visible.

Manually Modify The Luminance

- Select Apple > System Preferences on your Mac, and then select Displays in the sidebar. (Depth may require the user to navigate.)
- Adjust the luminance of your display by dragging the luminance slider to the right.

Potentially present alongside the display type linked to your Mac is a Contrast toggle, which can be utilized to modify the contrast of the display.

ADJUSTING THE VOLUME

To adjust the intensity setting on your Mac, perform one of the subsequent:

- Employ the volume controls via the Control Strip or the volume keys on your keyboard. To rapidly mute the volume, for instance, click.
- To access the Sound control, select Apple > System Settings from the sidebar if it is not visible in the menu bar. (You may be required to navigate down.) Select whether Sound should always be displayed in the menu bar or only when it is active by clicking the pop-up menu next to Sound on the right.
- Application volume controls should be utilized, such as in the application for Apple TV.

UTILIZE MOUSE AND TRACKPAD GESTURES

You can use gestures with an Apple trackpad or Magic Mouse in conjunction with a Mac to focus on documents, navigate through music or websites, rotate photographs, and access the Notification Centre, among other things.

Input Of Trackpad Gestures

For additional functions, use one or more fingertips to manipulate the trackpad's surface: click, touch, slide, and gesture. To navigate within pages of a document, for instance, utilize two fingertips to swipe left or right.

- To view a brief video displaying each trackpad gesture that is supported on your Mac, navigate to Apple > System Preferences > Trackpad in the sidebar. (Depth may require the user to navigate.)

Additionally, gestures can be disabled or modified via the Trackpad settings.

Mouse Movements

To interact with the mouse, one or more fingertips should be used to touch, slide, glide, or click on items. For instance, to navigate between pages of a document, use one finger to swipe left or right.

- Select Mouse ⬚ from the sidebar of the Apple menu > System Preferences to see a brief video exhibiting each mouse gesture that is supported on a Mac. (Depth may require the user to navigate.)

Additionally, gestures can be disabled or modified in the Mouse settings.

UTILIZE TOUCH ID

Touch ID can be used to unlock a Mac, and authorize transactions from the App Store, iTunes Store, as well as Apple Books, while creating web-based purchases with Apple Pay if present on a Mac or Magic Keyboard. Touch ID can also be used to enroll in certain third-party applications.

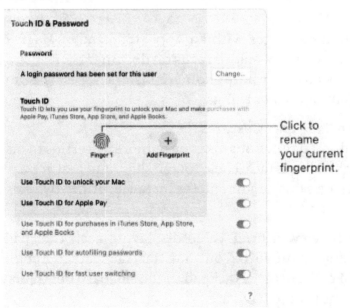

Touch ID and password configurations indicate that a fingerprint is prepared for use as a password to access the Mac.

Configure Touch ID

- Select Apple > System Preferences on your Mac, and then tap Touch ID & Password in the sidebar. (Depth may require the user to navigate.)
- After clicking "Add Fingerprint" and entering your password, proceed with the instructions displayed on-screen.

Touch ID-equipped Macs and Magic Keyboards feature a sensor situated in the upper-right corner of the device. Your user account can store a maximum of three fingerprints; on your Mac, you can store up to five fingerprints.

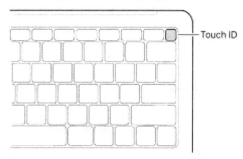

A touch-id-enabled keyboard in which the fingerprint sensor is located in the upper right quadrant.

- Select the desired way to utilize Touch ID:
- ✓ **Unlock your Mac**: When you revive this Mac from slumber, employ Touch ID to unlock it.
- ✓ **Apple Pay**: To finalize purchases made on this computer employing Apple Pay, employ Touch ID.
- ✓ **Apple App Store, iTunes Store, as well as Apple Books**: Use Touch ID to complete purchases from the Apple online stores on this Mac.
- ✓ **Password autofill**: Utilize Touch ID to populate credit card information and passwords and usernames automatically when prompted by Safari as well as other applications.
- ✓ **Rapid user switching**: To transition between accounts of users on this Mac, utilize Touch ID.

Eliminate Or Rename Biometrics

- Select Apple > System Preferences on your Mac, and then tap Touch ID & Password in the sidebar. (Depth may require the user to navigate.)
- Perform one of the following:
  ✓ To rename a fingerprint, input a name after clicking the text below the fingerprint.
  ✓ To delete a fingerprint, click on it, input the corresponding password, click Unlock, and then select Delete.

Unlock Your Computer, Login, Or Transfer Identities Using Touch ID

Before attempting to utilize Touch ID for these purposes, you must have previously signed into your Mac with your password.

- Unlock your Mac and select password-protected items by simply placing your index finger on Touch ID when prompted, or by rousing your Mac from slumber or accessing a password-protected item.
- To log in, select your name and then position your index finger on Touch ID in the logon interface.

Touch ID can only be used to activate user accounts that contain passwords; sharing-only users and visit users are unable to utilize it.

- To change users, select an alternative user via the rapid user toggling menu within the menu bar, and then touch ID with your finger.

In order to transition to a different user via Touch ID, two prerequisites must be met: rapid user switching must be enabled, and the target user must have previously authenticated to the Mac via password entry.

Utilize Touch ID For Purchases

- Your password is required to access your Mac.
- Invest in merchandise through one of them via the

Internet at Apple stores or by utilizing Apple Pay.
- When prompted, place the tip of your finger upon Touch ID.

Should you encounter issues with Touch ID?
- Touch ID will not recognize your fingerprint unless you ensure that your finger is dried and spotless before attempting again. Dry skin, moisture, moisturizers, or wounds may impede fingerprint recognition.
- If you are still prompted for your password, it is mandatory to input it upon starting your Mac for security purposes. Touch ID may require users to re-enter their password to continue functioning. For instance, after five unsuccessful biometric attempts and every 48 hours, users are required to re-enter their password.

PRINTING DOCUMENTS

Select a printer and configure print options that dictate how an image or document displays on the page that was printed using the Print dialogue on your Mac.

- While a document is active on your Mac, select File > Print or enter Command-P.

Upon opening the Print dialogue, a preview of the printed document appears.

It should be noted that the options displayed in the Print dialogue may vary depending on the printer and the application being utilized. If the subsequent instructions do not align with your current understanding, consult the application's documentation by selecting Help from the menu bar.

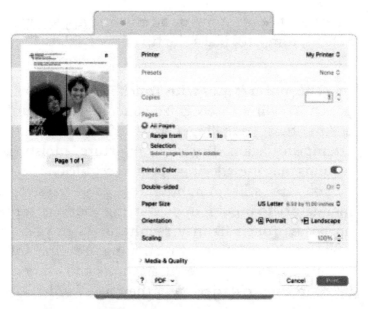

The Print dialogue presents a preview of the print project and print options.

To see a full-size preview within the Preview application, select Open PDF in Preview from the PDF pop-up menu.

- Once the parameters in the Print dialogue appear to be in the desired state, proceed by clicking Print. If not, proceed to step 3.
- To modify the printing options, select one of the prevalent print configurations listed below:
- ✓ Select the printer that you intend to utilize. If the printer is unavailable, an additional one can be added.
- ✓ Select a preset to have applied to your document by the printer. A preset comprises a collection of print configurations. While the default settings will suffice in the majority of situations, you can also select a set of preset settings from a previous printing task.
- ✓ Please indicate the number of copies that you require. To print every page of a document before the subsequent copy is printed, navigate to Paper Handling and choose "Collate Sheets."
- ✓ Define the range of pages that are to be printed. It

is possible to print an entire page or a specified range of pages. For instance, pages 6 through 9 of a 10-page document may be printed. The Selection icon can also be utilized to print a subset of the pages within the specified range. To select a page for printing, utilize the Preview sidebar and click the page designation. It is not required that the pages in which you choose form a continuous range. You may, for instance, choose to print pages 2 and 4 of a five-page document.

✓   Choose "Print in Colour" if your printer is equipped with this functionality. Disabling this option results in the output of documents in monochrome.

✓   Double-Sided: If your printer supports it, select On from the Double-Sided display menu and print on each side of the paper. This is also referred to as duplexing or two-sided printing. Additionally, by selecting On (Short Edge), the document can be configured to print with the binding available at the highest point of the page.

✓   Select an appropriate paper size for the document at hand. Select US Letter, for instance, when the printer is filled with 8.5-by-11-inch paper.

✓   To change the orientation between portrait as well as landscape, select the corresponding controls. The modification to your document is reflected in the sidebar of the preview pages.

✓   Input a scaling percentage to adapt the printed image from the dimensions of the paper. In the margin of the display pages, the modification is reflected.

✓   Select Print.

UTILIZE THE MACOS KEYPAD SHORTCUTS

Keyboard shortcuts are combinations of keys and values that can be used to complete duties more rapidly on a Mac. Keyboard shortcuts consist of simultaneously pressing one or more modifier keys (e.g., Control or Caps Lock) and a concluding key. One possible alternative to navigating to File > New Window in the menu bar is to utilize the Command and N keys.

In order to simplify the use of keyboard shortcuts, one may modify or disable them.

App-specific keyboard shortcuts may differ based on the language and keyboard configuration of the user's Mac. If the following shortcuts fail to function as expected, consult the menu bar for the application menus to locate the correct ones. Additionally, you can view your current keyboard layout, also known as an input source, using the Keyboard Viewer.

Investigate Keyboard Shortcuts On macOS

Shortcut keys are displayed adjacent to menu elements in macOS applications. Numerous auxiliary keys are shared by all applications.

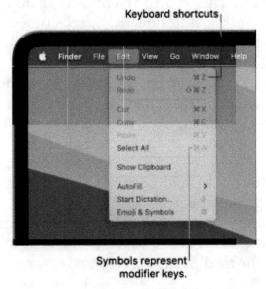

The Edit menu is visible in the Finder, accompanied by keyboard shortcuts.

Numerous macOS applications' user manuals contain a compilation of the most frequently utilized keyboard shortcuts for the application. For instance, see:

- Gestures and keyboard shortcuts for Safari
- Keyboard shortcut preview

- Disc Utility shortcuts for the keyboard

Additionally, the Apple Support article Mac keyboard shortcuts contains a wealth of keyboard shortcuts.

Execute Operations By Utilizing Keyboard Shortcuts

- Keep one or more modifier keys (including Caps Lock, Command, or Control) while simultaneously pressing the final key of the shortcut.

To paste copied text using the Command-V keyboard shortcut, for instance, hold down the Command key alongside the V key, then drop both keys.

Personalize The Keypad Shortcuts

Certain keyboard shortcuts are modifiable through the modification of key combinations.

- Select Apple > System Preferences on your Mac, then select Keyboard Shortcuts on the right (you might have to navigate down the sidebar to access Keyboard).
- Choose a category from the list located on the left, including Mission Control and Spotlight.

Selecting the Application Shortcuts category on the left will also allow you to modify keyboard shortcuts for particular applications.

- Choose the checkbox next to the desired shortcut in the list located on the right.
- To change the key combination, double-tap the existing key combination and then enter the desired key combination.

Each key type (letter keys, for instance) may only be utilized once when entering a key sequence.

- Reopening and quitting any running applications will cause the new keypad option to take effect.

Your new shortcut will not function if it is assigned to a keyboard shortcut that is already in use for a different command or application. Either the new shortcut or the existing shortcut must be modified.

To restore the original key combinations for each shortcut, navigate to Keyboard Settings > Keyboard Shortcuts > Restore Defaults (located in the bottom-left corner).

Stop Using A Keyboard Shortcut
Occasionally, the keyboard shortcut of an application and a macOS keyboard shortcut conflict. You may disable your macOS keypad shortcut if this occurs.

- Select Apple > System Preferences on your Mac, then select Keyboard Shortcuts on the right (you may need to navigate down the sidebar to access Keyboard).
- Choose a category from the list located on the left, including Mission Control and Spotlight.
- To disable a shortcut, uncheck the checkbox next to that shortcut in the list that appears on the right.

CHAPTER THREE

CUSTOMIZE YOUR MAC

Customization of a Mac is possible via system settings. You may, for instance, alter the wallpaper, select a light or dark appearance, and so forth.

Selectable Appearance choices on the right sidebar of the System Settings opening, which contains the Appearance settings.

The preferences menu organizes the available options on a Mac. In the Appearance settings, for instance, you will find options for configuring the Accent as well as Highlight colors.

- From the Apple menu, select System Settings, or tap the System Settings symbol in the Dock.
- Tap a configuration.

Varying by Mac as well as installed applications, the sidebar contains a selection of configuration options.

- Modify a given option.

For more information on the available options, the Help icon is typically present in the settings.

A red badge indicates that one or more actions are required if it appears on the System Settings symbol in the Dock. As an illustration, the badge becomes visible on the symbol in the Dock if iCloud functions are not entirely configured. Clicking the icon unveils the necessary settings to finalize the setup process.

Click the app's name in the navigation bar, then select Settings to modify configurations for an application, including Mail or Safari. Certain applications lack configuration options.

PERSONALIZE THE WALLPAPER

It is possible to modify the desktop image that is currently active. Utilize your images or select from a variety of colors and images supplied by Apple.

Sonoma Dynamic Wallpaper (Light) is selected on the right sidebar of the

System Settings window, which contains Wallpaper settings.

As an alternative to the current wallpaper, you can select an image to use as your desktop or folder by dragging the image onto the thumbnail of the sitting wallpaper.

- Select Wallpaper from the sidebar of the Apple menu > System Preferences on your Mac. (Diggesturing may be necessary.)
- Make your selection from the following categories of wallpapers:
✓ To select your images, use the Add Photo/Add Folder or Album controls.
✓ Utilizing the time of day in your current location, these images transform from brilliant to gloomy to create dynamic wallpapers.
✓ These still images depict aerials of the Earth, the landscape, the cityscape, and the ocean floor.
✓ Assign a time interval to these static images in Shuffle Aerials.
✓ Creative images are displayed in these still images.
✓ A solid-color background is applied to your desktop using these hues.
- Configure wallpaper settings.

Alternatives differ according to the wallpaper selected. Consider the following:

✓ Activate a slow-motion aerial using the static aerial of your backdrop as a screen saver.
✓ Determine the frequency of aerial shuffles.
✓ Opt for either the pale or dark renditions of the static wallpaper.
✓ Insert a custom hue.

Use the thumbnail located at the top of the Wallpaper settings to select a picture from the desktop or a folder to designate as your wallpaper.

Choose the photo, click the Share icon in the Photos interface, and then select Set Wallpaper to rapidly utilize a photo stored in the Photos application.

An online image may also be utilized as a desktop background. Make a desktop picture selection by control-clicking the pic in the browser window.

Connect Your Mac To A Screen Saver

When absent from your Mac or when additional privacy is required, you can utilize a screen saver to conceal the desktop.

The screen-saver configurations for macOS Sonoma (Light) are displayed in the sidebar of the System Settings window.

Personalize Your Mac's Screen Saver

- Locate the Screen Saver option in the sidebar of the Apple menu > System Preferences on your Mac. (Diggesturing may be necessary.)
- Choose an available category to choose a screen saver from:

✓ Slow-motion images are displayed on macOS.

✓ Slow-motion images of the Earth, Cityscape, Landscape, and Underwater provide dramatic perspectives.

✓ These slow-motion images, known as "shuffle aerials," update at the specified interval.

✓ In addition to displaying a message or "Word of the Day," these unique screen savers provide additional functionality.

· Configure preferences for your screen saver.

Options differ according to the selected screen saver. Consider the following:

✓ Utilize the screen saver's slow-motion aerial to activate a static aerial for your wallpaper.

✓ Determine the frequency of aerial shuffles.

✓ To shuffle your images, select a style.

Mac Screen Saver Activation And Deactivation

· Once your Mac has been inactive for the specified period, the screen saver will start automatically. Apple > System Preferences > Lock Screen in the sidebar to modify the maximum amount of time a Mac may remain idle before the screen saver is triggered. (Diggesturing may be necessary.) Change the parameters for the lock screen.

Movement of the pointer over the designated hot corner will initiate the screen saver immediately. Consult Employ heated corners.

Additionally, the screen saver can be activated via the Apple menu > Lock Screen.

· Touch the trackpad, move the cursor, or select any key to exit the screen saver and return to the desktop.

Utilize Your Mac Internet Accounts

By adding the accounts to your Mac, you can utilize Exchange, Google, Yahoo, and other online accounts in Mac applications.

Internet Account settings are where one adds and manages Internet accounts and account settings. Additionally, internet accounts can be added via applications that support them.

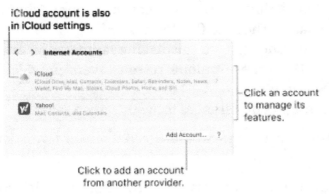

iCloud account is also in iCloud settings.

Click an account to manage its features.

Click to add an account from another provider.

Configure Internet Accounts using accounts that are already installed on the Mac.

iCloud accounts added through the iCloud configuration in Apple ID settings are also visible in the Internet Accounts configuration. Its parameters can be modified in either location.

Establish An Account Via A Program

Direct account addition is possible through the Calendar, Contacts, and Mail applications. Added accounts from these applications are displayed in the Internet Accounts settings. Before adding an account through an application, the account must be created on the provider's website.

- Select Add Account by clicking the app's name in the menu pane of the application on your Mac.

To illustrate, in Mail, select Mail > Add Account.

- After choosing the account provider, select Continue.

To incorporate an account from an unlisted provider, such as a corporate or educational calendar or email account, choose Other [Type of] Account, select Continue, and proceed with entering the details of the account that is prompted. Request the account provider for the details of the account if you are unaware of it.

- Input your account information, including the username and password.
- A dialogue box appears when you add an account that can be used by multiple applications; from this menu, you may choose which applications to associate with the account.

Establish A Connection Via The Internet Accounts Menu

Before adding an account through the Internet Accounts settings, the account needs to be created on the provider's website.

- Select Apple> System Preferences on your Mac, and then select Internet Accounts in the sidebar. (Depth may require the user to navigate.)
- After selecting Add Account from the menu on the right, select the account provider's name.

To incorporate an account from an unlisted provider, such as a corporate or educational calendar or email account, proceed as follows: click Add Other Account, select the account type, and input the requisite information for the account. Consult with the account provider if you are uncertain about the account type or information.

- Input your account data, including the username and password.
- A dialogue box appears when you add an account that can be used by multiple applications; from this menu, you can select which applications to associate with the account.

Modify Account Information And Features
- Select Apple > System Preferences on your Mac, and then select Internet Accounts in the sidebar. (Depth may require the user to navigate.)
- After selecting an account from the list on the right, perform one of the subsequent actions:
✓ **Toggle features**: Toggle functions on or off that you would like to utilize with the account.
✓ To modify account information, select the Details icon at

the top. In certain cases, the Details icon is absent because the account user name or email, a description, as well as additional information, are already displayed.

Cease Using The Account

- Select Apple > System Preferences on your Mac, and then select Internet Accounts @ in the sidebar. (Depth may require the user to navigate.)
- Select the desired account from the list on the right, and then perform one of the subsequent actions:
- ✓ To deactivate the account as well as remove its features, select Delete Account from the bottom menu, followed by OK.
- ✓ To deactivate a particular feature, locate the switch adjacent to that feature.

Data stored in your applications may be deleted if you delete your account or disable specific features. If you enable the feature or re-add the account, the data might be recovered. Inquire with the account provider if uncertain.

CREATING MEMOJI IN MESSAGES

It is possible to generate an individualized Memoji that corresponds to one's persona using macOS 11 or later. Then, convey your mood in your messages using Memoji.

Select a Memoji
sticker to use.

The Messages window, features a sidebar on the left that lists multiple conversations and a transcript on the right. You have the option to select an existing Memoji sticker or generate a new one by selecting Memoji Stickers from the Mobile Applications menu.

- On a Mac, within the Messages application, choose a conversation.
- Select the Memoji button by clicking the Stickers button after selecting the Apps button to the left of the text field.
- After selecting the Add button (for your initial Memoji) or the More button, proceed to adhere to the on-screen guidelines to generate and personalize your Memoji, commencing with the selection of apparel and extending to skin tone.
- Select Done.

ENLARGE TEXT AND OTHER ELEMENTS DISPLAYED ON A MAC

You can increase the scale of text and icons to improve their legibility or alter the screen resolution to enlarge the entire screen.

If you are having difficulty locating the indicator on the display, you can enlarge it or use the mouse tremor function to locate it rapidly. Ensure that the pointer is more visible.

Enlarge Every Element On The Screen

You ~~can~~ modify the resolution of your display to enlarge the size of every element on the screen.

- Select Apple > System Preferences on your Mac, and then select Displays in the sidebar. (Depth may require the user to navigate.)
- In the menu on the right, choose a resolution.

As the resolution decreases, the dimensions of all elements displayed on the screen enlarge.

Enlarge Text And Indicators Throughout Applications And System Components

You can modify the preferable reading scale for text across multiple applications, the desktop, and sidebars using a single slider.

- Select Apple > System Preferences on your Mac, then select Accessibility in the sidebar. (Depth may require the user to navigate.)
- Navigate to Text by clicking Display on the side, and then select "Text size." (You may be required to navigate down.)
- To enlarge the text size in the specified applications, sidebars, and the desktop (provided they are configured to Use Preferred Reading Size), move the slider to the right.

To modify the text size of any of the applications on the list, select a size from the pop-up menu that appears next to the application.

When an application is configured to Customized in App, its settings will contain a setting for a unique text size. Customizing the text size in System Preferences will override any adjustments made within the application.

An enlarged rendition of the text displayed on-screen can be accessed by hovering the pointer over it.

Enlarge Text For Specific Applications Or System Functions
Many applications allow you to customize the text size for that app only. Additionally, the text size of desktop labels and sidebars can be modified.

- You can alter the text size in certain applications, including Mail, Messages, and News, by pressing Command-Plus (+) or Command-Minus (–) while reading emails, messages, and articles.
- Additionally, you can configure the preferable text size for individual applications, such as Calendar, Mail, and Messages, via System Settings.
- To alter the text size on webpages, use Safari and select Command-Option-Plus (+) or Command-Option-Minus (—).
- Under the names of files and folders in the Finder, select View > Display View Options. Select a text size from the "Text size" pop-up menu that appears.
- It is not possible to adjust the text size in the Gallery view. Modify how folders are presented in the Finder.
- Control-click the desktop, select Show View Options, select "Text size" from the pop-up menu, and then enter the desired text size for desktop labels.
- Select Appearance from the sidebar that appears after navigating to System Preferences from the Apple menu (you might want to navigate down). Right-click the pop-up menu labeled "Sidebar icon size" and select "Large."

Enlarge Icons Representing Specific Applications Or System Functions

The icon size of items in the Finder, on the desktop, and in sidebars can be modified.

- In the Finder window, select View > Display View Options. In both the Icon and List views, select a larger symbol size. You have the option to select a larger thumbnail dimension in Gallery View.

Note: The icon size cannot be modified in the Column view. Modify how folders are presented in the Finder.

- Select Show View Options by performing a control-click on the desktop, and then dragging the "Icon size" slider to the right.
- Select Appearance from the sidebar that appears after navigating to System Preferences from the Apple menu (you might have to navigate down). Right-click the pop-up menu labeled "Sidebar icon size" and select "Large."

CONFIGURING A FOCUS

Utilize Focus when you must maintain concentration and minimize interruptions. A Focus can be utilized to suspend and silence all notifications, restrict access to specific ones, such as those from colleagues regarding an essential project, or enable only those. You can also inform contacts that you have deactivated notifications to indicate that you are occupied.

The focus parameters display the Work Focus configuration. The list of individuals and applications whose notifications are permitted while Work Focus is active appears at the top. At the midpoint is a time-based schedule that engages the Work Focus automatically. A Calendar Focus Filter appears at the bottom.

Need to deactivate all notifications immediately? Activate the Do Not Disturb focus option in the Control Centre.

REPLACE OR ADD A FOCUS

- Select Apple > System Preferences on your Mac, then select Focus in the sidebar. (Depth may require the user to navigate.)
- Perform one of the following actions on the right:
- ✓ To include a predefined focus, select Add Focus followed by the desired focus, such as Work or Gaming.
- ✓ To generate a personalized focus, select Add Focus followed by Custom. After entering a name, choosing an icon and color, click OK. As an illustration, one could establish a Study Focus. Ten can be created in total.
- ✓ To modify a custom focus, select it from the list by clicking

on it. To modify the Focus's name, color, or emblem, click the icon.

✓ To unload a focus, select it from the list and proceed by clicking Delete Focus located at the bottom of the window.

A personalized Focus is removed. A specified Focus, such as Mindfulness or Reading, is eliminated from the roster; however, it remains accessible for subsequent addition.

Maintaining Focus on all Apple devices ensures that any modifications performed on the Mac are automatically replicated on the other devices.

DETERMINE WHICH NOTIFICATIONS TO ENABLE

Notifications from specific individuals and applications, time-sensitive notifications, or phone call notifications that have been received on your Mac are among the customizable options for which notifications are displayed while a Focus is active.

Notifications from certain applications, including Calendar, are time-sensitive. Choose the option to permit these notifications to ensure that you receive them.

- Select Apple > System Preferences on your Mac, then select Focus in the sidebar. (Depth may require the user to navigate.)
- Right-click a Focus option.
- Navigate to Allow Notifications, select Allowed People, and then complete one of the following tasks (when complete, click Done):

✓ Select Allow Some People from the pop-up menu adjacent to Notifications to enable notifications from specific individuals. After clicking the Add People icon, one or more contacts can be selected. As an illustration, for the Games Focus, one might choose their customary companions in multiplayer games.

Simply hover the cursor over the individual you wish to remove from the list, and then select the Remove icon.

✓   Select Silence Some People from the pop-up menu adjacent to Notifications to disable notifications from specific individuals. After clicking the Add People icon, any number of contacts can be selected.

Simply hover the cursor over the individual you wish to remove from the list, and then select the Remove icon.

✓ Select an option from the pop-up menu that appears next to "Allow calls from," then enable phone call notifications. You have the option of receiving call notifications from the following groups: only authorized individuals, individuals from your Contacts list, or individuals from your Favourites on your iPhone.

✓ Enable notifications for repetitive phone calls: Click "Allow repeated calls" to be notified when an individual makes two or more calls within three minutes.

• Navigate to Allow Notifications, select Allowed Apps, and then complete one of the following tasks (when complete, click Done):

✓ Permit notifications from specific applications by selecting Allow Some Apps from the Notifications pop-up menu. Following the selection of one or more applications, click the Add icon. For the Work Focus, for instance, you might restrict notifications to only those applications that are essential for your work.

Click the Remove icon after hovering the cursor over the application you wish to remove from the list.

✓   To disable notifications from specific applications, select Silence Some Apps from the Notifications pop-up menu. Following the selection of one or more applications, click the Add icon.

Click the Remove icon after hovering the cursor over the application you wish to remove from the list.

✓   Enable notifications for tasks or events that

demand your immediate attention: Enable "Time-sensitive notifications." (In the Notifications settings, ensure that you likewise select the option that permits applications to send these alerts.)

By default, the Gaming Focus feature is configured to activate whenever a game device is linked to a Mac. To be notified while the Gaming Focus is active, specific individuals or applications must be included.

AUTOMATICALLY SCHEDULE A FOCUS TO SWITCH ON OR OFF

It is possible to programmatically activate or deactivate a Focus at specified intervals, upon entering or exiting particular locations, or upon launching or closing specific applications.

- Select Apple > System Preferences on your Mac, then select Focus in the sidebar. (Depth may require the user to navigate.)
- Right-click a Focus option.
- Navigate to Schedule Setup, select Add Schedule, and then perform one of the following:
  - ✓ Create a time-based schedule by selecting Time, entering a start and end date, and selecting the desired days of the week before clicking Done.

    To modify a time-based schedule, select it, make the necessary adjustments, and then select "Done."

    To cease employing a time-dependent schedule temporarily, select it, deactivate Schedule at the highest point of the window, and then select Done.

  - ✓ To create a schedule based on location, press Location, input the name of a location into the Search field, and then select Done.

A Focus that is programmed according to your location will activate upon your arrival at the specified location as well as deactivate upon your departure.

To stop employing a location-based schedule temporarily, select it, deactivate Automation at the window's top, and then select Done.

To utilize a location, Location Services need to be enabled in the Privacy settings.

✓ To create an application-based schedule, select an application by clicking Done after entering its name in the Search field and clicking App.

A focus that is scheduled following an application becomes active upon opening the app and deactivates upon closing it or transitioning to an alternative application.

To stop working with an app-based schedule temporarily, select it, deactivate Automation at the window's top, and then select Done.

MODIFY APPLICATION BEHAVIOUR

Customize the behavior of Calendar, Mail, Messages, and Safari when a Focus is enabled by adding a Focus filter. For instance, when using the Personal Focus, you can conceal your work calendar while in the Work Focus, or select a set of Tab Groups to show up in Safari while in the Personal Focus.

- Select Apple > System Preferences on your Mac, then select Focus in the sidebar. (Depth may require the user to navigate.)
- Right-click a Focus option.
- Navigate to Focus Filters, select Add Filter, and then perform one of the subsequent:

✓ To configure a Focus filter for Calendar, navigate to Calendar, select the calendars that should be displayed during the Focus, and then click Add.

✓ To create a Focus filter for Mail, navigate to Mail, select the email accounts that should be visible during the Focus, and then click Add.

✓ To configure a Focus filter for Messages, navigate to Messages, enable Filter by People List, and then select Add.

✓ To configure a Focus filter for Safari, navigate to Safari, click Choose next to the Tab Group, pick the Tab Group that should be visible while this filter is active, toggle "Open external links in your Focus Tab Group" to the desired state, and finally click Add.

After configuring a Focus Filter, it is possible to modify it or discontinue its use temporarily. Select Apple > System Preferences, then click Focus 🌙 in the sidebar, select a specific focus, and finally select the desired focus filter. To activate, deactivate, or modify the parameters for the Focus Filter, utilize the icon located at the top of the window. Click Done when the process is complete.

Select Apple > System Preferences > Focus, then click Focus 🌙 in the sidebar, select a Focus, select the desired Focus Filter, and finally click Delete Application Filter at the bottom of the window to remove the filter.

MAINTAIN CURRENT FOCUS PARAMETERS ON ALL APPLE DEVICES

Any adjustments you make to Focus while signed in with the same Apple ID across each of your Apple devices are synchronized with those gadgets. Specifically, activating or deactivating a Focus on one device will cause it to be similarly activated or deactivated on all of your other gadgets.

- Select Apple > System Preferences on your Mac, then select Focus in the sidebar. (Depth may require the user to navigate.)
- On the right, toggle "Share across devices" on or off. (By default, the option is enabled.)

SPECIFY YOUR STATUS OF FOCUS

You can enable apps to notify acquaintances who give you messages that you have deactivated notifications (they will no longer be able to see which Focus you are employing). Despite this, they may choose to notify you if the matter is critical.

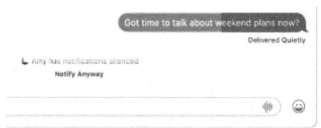

Discussion via Messages. The Messages option signifies that a message was delivered inaudibly, as the recipient has disabled notifications. Clicking the "Notify Anyway" link below will cause the recipient to resend the message.

- Select Apple > System Preferences on your Mac, then select Focus in the sidebar. (Depth may require the user to navigate.)
- Opt for "Focus status."
- Activate "Share Focus status."
- Deactivate each Focus below Share From to indicate which individuals are permitted to share while your notifications are muted.

HOW TO CONFIGURE SCREEN TIME

Enable Screen Time on your Mac to monitor the amount of time you spend on it and other gadgets. Screen Time enables the display of reports detailing the usage of applications, the frequency of device operation, and the number of notifications received.

- Select Apple > System Preferences on your Mac, then select Screen Time in the sidebar. (Depth may require the user to navigate.)
- Select yourself if you are a parent or guardian in a Family Sharing group by selecting the Family Member pop-up menu on the right.
- To activate App & Website Activity, navigate to App & Website Activity > Turn On.
- Scroll down and click the back icon before activating one of the subsequent options:
  ✓ If you want Screen Time statistics to incorporate time spent on other devices that are also signed in with the same Apple ID, enable this option.

This option is accessible exclusively when an Apple ID is in use.

✓ Enabling the Lock Screen Time Settings option will entail the need for a passcode to access Screen Time settings while permitting an extension of time when existing limits expire.

You will be prompted to convert the administrator account of the family member to a standard account if they have one.

- Additionally, the following can be modified via Screen Time settings:

✓ Navigate to Application & Website Activity, Notifications, or Pickups to observe the utilization of your device and application.

✓ Create an inactivity schedule by selecting inactivity.

✓ In the Application Limits menu, configure time limits for websites as well as applications.

✓ Select Always Allowed applications, followed by always-accessible applications.

✓ By selecting Screen Distance, you can be notified when you approach a device too closely.

✓ After selecting Communication Limits, configure communication limits.

✓ Select Communication Safety, followed by the scan for sensitive images option.

✓ Configure content and privacy restrictions by selecting Content & Privacy.

HOW TO ENTER TEXT BY DICTATION

Dictation enables users to input text simply by speaking in any location with a typing interface.

For supported languages, dictation queries are processed locally on a Mac with Apple silicon; an internet connection is not mandatory. Donned text entered into a search box may be transmitted to the search provider for search processing.

Moreover, text of any length can be dictated without the occurrence of a timeout. Dictation can be deactivated either manually or automatically after 30 seconds of silence.

When dictating in a language that is not supported by the device or on an Intel-based Mac, the dictated utterances are transmitted to Apple for processing.

Voice Control enables you to dictate text and operate your Mac employing your voice as opposed to the keyboard and trackpad.

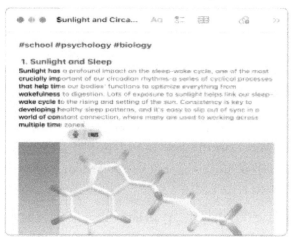

The dictation tools are illustrated in a note with dictated text.

Enable Dictation

- In the sidebar of the Apple menu > System Preferences, select Keyboard on your Mac. (Depth may require the user to navigate.)
- Navigate to Dictation on the right, and activate it. When prompted, select the Enable button.
- When asked how Siri and Dictation could be improved, select one of what following options:
- ✓ To grant Apple permission to store audio recordings of your Mac's Siri and Dictation interactions, navigate to Share Audio Recordings. Apple may examine a preserved audio sample.
- ✓ Avoid sharing audio recordings by selecting the "Not Now"

option.

Should you subsequently decide to share or discontinue sharing audio recordings, navigate to Apple > System Preferences > Privacy & Security in the sidebar. (You may be required to scroll down.) Navigate to Analytics & Upgrades on the right, then toggle the Improve Siri & Dictation option to the desired state.

It is possible to remove audio interactions at any time; they are linked with a random identifier and are older than six months.

- Select a language and dialect by clicking the Edit icon adjacent to Languages in order to dictate in a different language. (Select a language to eliminate it.)

Voice Over Text
- In a Mac application, position the insertion point at the desired location for the dictated text to manifest.
- If the Microphone key is present in the series of function keys, select Edit > Start Dictation or utilize the Dictation keyboard shortcut.

Note: To initiate dictation, press as well as release the Microphone key. To activate Siri, hold down the Microphone key (Siri must be enabled).

- Dictate your text when a microphone symbol shows above or beneath a marked cursor, or when you receive the tone that indicates your Mac is prepared for dictation.

Typing text whilst dictating is possible on a Mac with Apple silicon; there is no requirement to interrupt dictation. In order to keep on dictating, the microphone symbol vanishes during typing as well as reappears once the user has ceased working.

- Employ one or more of the following to put in an emoji or punctuation mark, or to execute basic formatting operations:
  ✓ Pronounce an emoji's name, such as "car emoji" or "heart emoji."

✓ Pronounce the punctuation mark's name, as in "exclamation mark."

✓ Pronounce "new line" or "new paragraph" (which is equivalent to once and twice tapping the Return key, respectively). A new line or paragraph will be appended once the dictation is complete.

Please be advised that Dictation will automatically incorporate commas, periods, as well as question marks while you dictate in approved languages. Tap Keyboard in the toolbar of the Apple menu > System Preferences to disable this function. (Scroll down if necessary.) Navigate to Dictation on the right and deactivate Auto-punctuation.

- If you have configured Dictation to support multiple languages and wish to toggle between them while dictating, simply select the desired language by clicking the language icon adjacent to the microphone or the Globe key.
- Select the Dictation keypad shortcut or the Escape symbol when you are finished. Dictation ceases automatically after thirty seconds pass with no speech detected.

Ambiguous text is highlighted in blue. You may receive the result "flour" when you intend to type "flower." In such a case, choose an alternative by clicking the underlined word. Additionally, the precise text can be typed or dictated.

Configure The Dictation Shortcut Keystroke

You have the option of selecting an existing Dictation keypad shortcut or developing your own.

If the Microphone icon is present in the series of function buttons, you can employ your keyboard shortcut or select it to initiate dictation.

- In the sidebar of the Apple menu > System Preferences, select Keypad on your Mac. (Depth may require the user to navigate.)

- To launch Dictation, navigate to Dictation on your right, select a shortcut from the menu that appears next to Shortcut, and then click Dictation.

To generate a custom shortcut not already in the list, select Customize and then strike the desired keys. One possible approach is to select Option Z.

Take note: Depending on the version of your Mac, the "Press the fn key to" or "Click the Globe key to" option in Keypad settings might immediately alter when you select a Dictation keypad shortcut. As an illustration, selecting the Dictation Shortcut choice "Click Fn (Function) Key Twice" automatically modifies the keypad Settings option to " Begin Dictation (Press Fn Twice)."

To obtain further assistance regarding the keypad's options, navigate to the Keypad settings and select the Help icon.

Alter The Microphone Used During Dictation
In the keyboard settings, the microphone's source indicates what gadget is presently being used by your Mac to receive dictation.

- In the sidebar of the Apple menu > System Preferences, select Keypad on your Mac. (Depth may require the user to navigate.)
- After navigating to Dictation on the correct side and selecting the desired microphone for Dictation from the menu that appears next to "Microphone source," proceed to select the desired microphone.

Your Mac will listen to the device you most frequently employ for dictation if you select Automatic.

Disable Dictation
- In the side panel of the Apple menu > System Preferences, select Keypad on your Mac. (Depth may require the user to navigate.)
- Navigate to Dictation on the side, and deactivate it.

HOW TO SEND AN EMAIL

Emails can be sent, saved as drafts, and scheduled for future delivery.

Before sending an email, the Mail application requires the addition of at least one email account.

Dial An Email

- On a Mac, launch the Mail application and select the New Message option from the Mail toolbar.
- Enter the intended recipient's email address in the To field.

Additionally, from the Contacts application, you can send emails to an array of email addresses or conceal the email addresses of all recipients to secure their privacy.

- In the Subject field, enter the subject matter of your email.
- Type your message into the Message field (located beneath the subject).

You possess the ability to add formatting to the text of the email as well as attach images as well as other files to it.

- Navigate to the Send menu.

Develop A Draft

- Ensure that the message you wish to save is currently open in the Mail application on your Mac.
- Navigate to File > Save.

Additionally, you may dismiss the message window and select Save in the resulting dialogue.

You can locate your manuscript in the Drafts inbox (accessible via the Favourites tab or through the Mail sidebar) when you wish to access it again.

Plan To Send An Email

A menu containing various options for delivering an email, including Forward Now, Forward 8:00 AM Tomorrow, as well as Send Later, within the message window.

Perform one or more of the actions that follow on the Mac using the Mail application:

- To set up an email, select a time from the menu that appears adjacent to the Send icon, or select Send Later to establish a time and a date.

The email is displayed in the Mail sidebar's Send Later folder.

- To modify an email's appointed time, select Edit from the Send Later mailbox and double-tap the email in the upper-right corner.
- To halt the transmission of a scheduled email, locate the message in the Send Later folder and proceed by clicking the Delete icon.

SENDING A MESSAGE

Messages on a Mac need not be tedious. You may send messages to an individual, a group, or a business after configuring your Mac. These messages can contain text, images, animated effects, as well as more. One can articulate oneself through a multitude of means:

- Tapbacks.
- Videos and photos.
- Insert illustrations, photographs, and scans (from an iPhone or iPad.
- Image and sticker usage: Refer to Send stickers, Utilize #images, and Create a Memoji.
- Regarding audio messages.
- Effects on messages.

Tapback   Image   Memoji

Click the Apps button to add   Live Sticker
photos, videos, #images,
stickers, and message effects.

The Messages window, features a sidebar on the left that lists multiple conversations and a transcript on the right. The transcript emphasizes several elements: a Live Sticker located in the lower-right corner, a Tapback above a pinned discussion on the left, and an image and Memoji on the right. To add photographs, videos, imagery, emoticons, and message effects, select the Apps button located at the bottom of the display.

- To write a new message within the Messages application on your Mac, select the Compose icon or utilize the Touch Bar.
- Please provide the full name, email address, or telephone number of the intended recipient in the "To" field. Messages suggest addresses that match those in your Contacts application ▦or from recipients to whom you have previously sent texts as your input.

Additionally, the Add option is located to the far right of the To field. By selecting a contact from the list, the phone number or email address can be accessed

Please be advised that if you are limited to communicating via messages with specific individuals, an hourglass symbol⌛ will show up next to their names.

- In the field located at the bottom of the opening, enter what you want to say. If accessible, typing recommendations may be utilized.

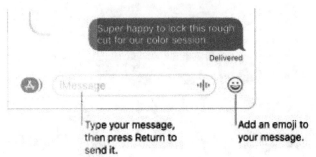

Type your message, then press Return to send it.

Add an emoji to your message.

The transcript is displayed within the Messages window, using the message field situated at the window's bottom.

"Instruct your mother that I will be late" is an example of a Siri command.

- To transmit the message, utilize the Return key on the keypad or select the Send icon.

CHAPTER FOUR

HOW TO MAKE AND RECEIVE VIDEO
CALLS USING FACETIME

FaceTime video conversations allow participants to both see and hear one another via a gadget made by Apple that satisfies the specified criteria. FaceTime video communications utilize the Wi-Fi connection of your Mac.

Enter callers straight into the To field or select them from the Suggested list in the new FaceTime window.

ENGAGE IN A FACETIME WEBINAR

- On a Mac, launch the FaceTime application and select New FaceTime.
- Enter the desired recipient's email address or telephone number into the New FaceTime window. Potentially, you must select Return.

If the individual is in the Contacts, you may choose them from the Suggested list or input their name directly. Additionally, contacts can be added coming from the New FaceTime interface.

- Navigate to FaceTime or employ the Touch Bar.

Using Siri, say "FaceTime mom." Acquire knowledge of using Siri.

INTERACT WITH A FACETIME VIDEO SESSION

Accepting communications while signed in and FaceTime enabled is possible regardless of the presence of an active FaceTime session.

Perform one or more of the following on the Mac when a notification shows up in the upper-right corner of the display:

- To answer an incoming call, press Accept.
- To grant a video call as an audio call, select Answer as Audio from the drop-down menu next to Accept. During phone or audio conversations, the camera is turned off automatically.
- To terminate the current call and accept an incoming call, select terminate and accept.
- To reject a contact, select Decline.

An alternative option is to create a reminder or send a text message by selecting the down arrow adjacent to Decline.

You can block a contact whose number you do not wish to receive further communications from.

You can continue a call after it has begun or share a connection to it.

DECLINE FACETIME VIDEO SESSION

You may decline communications while signed in as well as FaceTime is enabled, regardless of whether the application is currently active.

Perform one or more of the following on the Mac when an alert shows up in the upper-right corner of the display:

- To reject a contact, select Decline.

The recipient observes that you are not reaching out to receive a contact.

You can block a contact whose number you do not wish to receive further communications from.

- To send a message as well as decline a call using iMessage, select Reply with Message from the drop-down menu next to Decline, enter your message, and finally select Send. To use iMessage, both yourself and the receiver must be signed in.
- To decline a call and schedule a follow-up reminder, select the down arrow adjacent to Decline and then enter the desired wait time. You will be notified when the time arrives; clicking on the alert will take you to the reminder, where you can then select the link to initiate the call.

ENDING A FACETIME VIDEO CALL

Simply hover the cursor throughout the call window and select the Leave Call icon (or utilize the Touch Bar) to terminate the conversation.

CHAPTER FIVE

APPS

LAUNCHING APPLICATIONS

It is possible to simultaneously run and display multiple applications on a Mac. This is particularly beneficial for frequently used applications, like Safari or Mail.

To launch an application on a Mac in the shortest amount of time, select its icon from the Dock.

The indicator for Safari in the Dock.

If the application's icon is not present in the Dock, alternative methods exist for launching it on a Mac:

- After selecting the Launchpad indicator ⁚⁚⁚ from the Dock, select an application icon.
- Utilize Siri to launch an application on your behalf."
- Press Return after selecting Spotlight from the menu bar and entering the name of the desired application in the search field. Refer to Search using Spotlight.
- Select the application from the Apple menu > Recent Items if you have recently used it.
- Double-tap the application after selecting Applications from the sidebar of the Finder window via the icon for the Finder in the Dock.

Organize And Relocate Application Windows On A Mac

When an application or the Finder is launched on a Mac, a window appears on the desktop. Active at any given moment is a single application; the menu bar displays the app's name (in bold) and its menus.

A desktop example containing multiple open windows but just one active application.

Certain applications, such as Mail or Safari, permit the simultaneous opening of multiple windows or windows of various categories. On macOS, there are multiple methods for managing active app windows and closing any or all of them.

Merge, Reposition, And Align App Windows

Perform one or more of the following on your Mac:

- To manually relocate a window, simply drag its contents by its title bar to the desired location. Certain windows are immobile.
- To relocate a window to one side of the display, hold down the Option key while hovering the mouse pointer over the green icon located in the upper-left corner of the window. From the resulting menu, select Move Window to Left Side of Display or Move Window to Right Side of Display. While the window occupies that portion of the screen, the Dock and menu bar remain visible.

To revert the window to its original size and position, hover the mouse pointer over the green icon while holding down the Option key, and then select Revert.

- Align windows by dragging one window near another; the

windows will align without overlapping as the window approaches the other. It is possible to arrange multiple apertures in an adjacent space.

To resize adjacent windows to the same dimensions, drag the desired boundary; it will cease aligning with the adjacent window's edge as it approaches it.

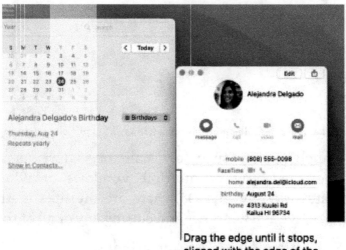

Drag the edge until it stops, aligned with the edge of the adjacent window.

By dragging the outermost part of one window toward another till it stops, two windows can be aligned along one side. This window is in alignment with the adjacent window.

- Select Window > Merge All Windows within the application to combine its windows into a single tabbed window. Mail combines only the active type of window if it contains multiple window types (e.g., the viewer window as well as the new message window).

To restore a tab to its original state as a distinct window, drag the tab out of the window or select Window > Move Tab to New Window.

Reduce Or Maximize Application Windows

Perform one or more of the following actions in a window on your Mac:

- To maximize an application window, select as well as hold

the green icon in the upper-left corner while holding down the Option key. Select the option to revert the window size by clicking the icon once more.

- Additionally, you may maximize an application's window by double-clicking its title bar, provided that the Zoom option is enabled in the Desktop & Dock settings.

To minimize a window, select Command-M or select the yellow minimize icon located in the upper-left corner of the window.

In the Desktop & Dock settings, it is possible to configure a window to minimize when the title bar is double-clicked.

A majority of windows are resizable manually. Expand an additional of the window by dragging its edge (the top, bottom, or sides) or by double-clicking on that edge.

Move Between Application Windows Rapidly
Perform one or more of the following actions on your Mac:

- To exit the current application, click Command-Tab.
- To navigate through all open applications, hold down the Command key while holding down the Tab key. From there, select the desired application by pressing the Left or Right arrow key. Discard the Command keystroke.

While browsing through the applications, if you alter the way you think as well as do not wish to transfer apps, select and hold the Period or Esc key.

Close One Or More Windows Associated With An Application
Perform one or more of the following actions on your Mac:

- If you want to close a single window, select Command-W or select the red Close icon located in the upper-left corner of the window.
- To close all open application windows, select Option-Command-W.

Apps that have one or more windows closed do not terminate;

the application remains operational, as indicated by the dot located beneath its icon in the Dock. To exit the application, type Command-.

<h2 style="text-align:center">FULL-SCREEN APPLICATION</h2>

Numerous applications on your Mac support full-screen operation, which allows 'you to work without interface interruptions while maximizing the use of every available inch of the screen.

- Navigate to the green icon located in the upper-left quadrant of the window on your Mac. From the resulting menu, select Enter Full Screen, or press the button.

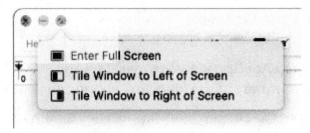

The menu displays when the green icon in the upper-left corner of a window is hovered over. From top to bottom, the menu contains the following options: Enter Full Screen, Tile Window to Left of Screen, as well as Tile Window to Right of Screen.

- While in full-screen mode, perform any of the actions listed below:
- ✓ To enable or disable the menu bar, move the cursor toward or away from the screen's top. Selecting the option to conceal and display the navigation bar on the entire screen results in the menu bar remaining visible at all times.
- ✓ To display or conceal the Dock, simply move the cursor to or from its location.
- ✓ Navigate between applications in full screen: Using three or four fingers, swipe to the left or right on the trackpad, depending on the trackpad settings.
- To exit the application in full-screen mode, hover over the green button once more and select Exit Full Screen from the resulting menu, or click the button itself.

Maximizing the window allows you to work in a larger space without reverting to full-screen mode; while the window enlarges, the menu bar, as well as Dock, remain visible.

While an app is in full-screen mode, it is possible to rapidly select another app to utilize in Split View. To access Mission Control, press the Control-Up Arrow (or slide up with three to four fingers), then drag the window from Mission Control to the full-screen app's thumbnail in the Spaces bar, followed by a click on the Split View thumbnail. Additionally, thumbnails of apps can be dragged onto each other in the Spaces interface.

UTILIZE APPLICATIONS SPLIT VIEW

Numerous applications on your Mac support Split View, allowing you to simultaneously use two applications side by side.

In Split View, the Mail application is on the left as well and
the Photos application is on the right.

- Press the green icon located in the upper-left corner of the window on your Mac. From the resulting menu, select Tile Window to Left of Display or Tile Window to Right of Display.

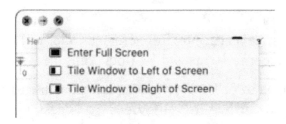

The menu displays when the green icon in the upper-left corner of a window is hovered over. From top to bottom, the menu contains the following options: Enter Full Screen, Tile Window to Left of Display, as well as Tile Window to Right of Screen.

- Select the second application you wish to utilize on the opposite side of the display.

A new workspace is created for the Split View on the desktop.

- Perform even one of what follows in Split View:
✓ To enable or disable the menu bar, move the cursor toward or away from the screen's top. Selecting the option to conceal and display the menu bar on the entire screen results in the menu bar remaining visible at all times.
✓ To display or conceal the Dock, simply move the cursor to or from its location.
✓ Display or conceal the title and toolbar of a window: Move the pointer toward or away from the highest point of the display after clicking the window.
✓ To enlarge a single side, hover the cursor across the separator bar positioned in the center and proceed by dragging it to the left or right. Select the separator bar twice to revert to the initial dimensions.
✓ To change sides, drag a window to the opposite side using its toolbar as well as the title.
✓ Employ an alternative application on one side: Select Replace Tiled Window by hovering the cursor over the green icon in the upper-left corner of the application window, after which you can select the desired window to use in its place. Clicking the desktop will return you to the present window if you choose not to replace it.

✓ To relocate an application window to the desktop, select Move Window to Desktop after hovering the cursor over the green icon in the upper-left corner of the window. The application is launched from the desktop.

To access the app that was previously displayed in Split View in its own dedicated space, navigate to Mission Control and hold the Control-Up Arrow (or slide up with three or four fingers). From there, select the app in the Spaces tab to return to it.

✓ To open an application window in full-screen mode, select Make Window Full Screen after hovering the cursor over the green icon in the upper-left quadrant of the window.

To access the app that was previously displayed in Split View in its own dedicated space, navigate to Mission Control and hold the Control-Up Arrow (or slide up with three or four fingers). From there, select the application in the Spaces tab to return to it.

While an app is in full-screen mode, it is possible to easily switch to another app for use in Split View. To access Mission Control, press the Control-Up Arrow (or swipe upward using three to four fingers), then drag a window from Mission Control to the full-screen application's thumbnail in the Spaces bar, followed by clicking on the Split View thumbnail. In the Spaces bar, you may also place an application thumbnail onto a different one.

To utilize applications in Split View across multiple displays, enable "Displays have distinct spaces" in the Desktop & Dock settings.

DESKTOP ORGANIZATION USING STAGE MANAGER

Maintain the active application in the foreground and a clutter-free desktop on your Mac by utilizing Stage Manager. For easy access, your most recently utilized applications are systematically organized on the left side of the display, whereas the window you are currently utilizing is situated in the screen's center.

Window overlaps, resizing, and arrangement to create the

ideal layout. In Stage Manager, you can also organize multiple applications on the display to collaborate as a unit. All applications in a group launch in the center of the display when the user transitions to a group.

A desktop displaying Stage Manager, with a single app window in the screen's center and a catalog of recently used applications for four applications on the left.

Toggle Stage Manager Between On And Off

You can effortlessly transition between Stage Manager as well as traditional windows to utilize the approach that is most appropriate for the task at hand.

Perform one or more of the following on the Mac:

- Select Apple > System Preferences on your Mac, followed by Desktop & Dock in the sidebar. (Depth may require the user to navigate.) To enable or disable Stage Manager, navigate to Desktop & Stage Manager on the right.
- Within the menu bar, select Control Centre, then Stage Manager to enable or disable it.

Employ Stage Manager

Perform one or more of the following actions on your Mac:

- To switch between applications, tap an app located on the

left part of the display.
- Windows may be repositioned, resized, or overlapped to accommodate the user's workflow.
- To add an app to a group of applications in the center of the display, drag the mobile application from the left side of the display to that location.
- Ungroup applications: To remove an application from a group, drag it to the left side of the display.

The list of applications on the left is concealed if "Show most recent applications in Stage Manager" is deactivated in the Stage Manager settings. To display it, move the pointer to the far left margin of the display.

Display Or Conceal The Stage Manager Option In The Menu

The Stage Manager is consistently accessible within the Control Centre. You have the option to display it in the menu bar as well.

- Select Apple > System Preferences on your Mac, then select Control Centre in the sidebar. (Depth may require the user to navigate.)
- On the right, beside Stage Manager, select Show in Menu Bar or Don't Show in Menu Bar from the pop-up menu that appears.

Modify Stage Manager Configurations

- Select Apple > System Preferences on your Mac, followed by Desktop & Dock in the sidebar. (Depth may require the user to navigate.)
- Navigate to Stage Manager and Desktop on the right.
- Inspect the following checkboxes in addition to "Show Items":
✓ Display desktop elements on the desktop.
✓ Display desktop elements in Stage Manager when it is activated.

Disabling this option results in the desirability of desktop items; to access them, simply select the desktop.

- Select an option from the "Click wallpaper to reveal desktop" pop-up menu that appears:
  - ✓ Clicking the wallpaper always repositions all windows to make room for the widgets and desktop elements.
  - ✓ Clicking the backdrop in Stage Manager only causes all windows to vanish, allowing the desktop items as well as widgets to be displayed.
- Toggle Stage Manager between on and off.
- In or out of the "Show recent applications in Stage Manager" setting.

When this option is deactivated, recently used applications are concealed; to temporarily reveal them, hover the cursor over the left margin of the display.

- Select an option from the "Show windows from an application" pop-up menu that appears:
  - ✓ **Completely at Once**: While in an application, all of the accessible windows for that program are displayed.
  - ✓ **Display one at a time:** Upon switching to an application, only your most recently utilized window will be displayed.

While this choice is deactivated, clicking the application again from the left will launch the following accessible window.

INSTALLATION OF THE APPS STORE PURCHASES

There exist multiple methods for installing and reinstalling applications acquired using an Apple ID.

All purchases made through the App Store are associated with the user's Apple ID and are non-transferable to an alternative Apple ID. Consistently sign in with the same Apple ID when making purchases on a Mac, iPhone, iPad, or another device, so that you can access all of your store purchases as well as download the latest versions from this Mac.

Install Applications Acquired On An Additional Device

Any application purchased with an Apple ID can be installed on a different device.

- Select your name in the bottom-left area of the App Store on your Mac, or Sign In if you have not yet done so.
- After locating the purchased application that you wish to download, select Download.

Hold the cursor over the progress indicator of an active download to view its pace and status.

Download Applications That Were Purchased On A Separate Device Automatically

- Select the Application Store > Settings from the App Store on your Mac.
- Choose "Download applications purchased on other gadgets automatically."

Reinstall Applications

You may reinstall an application you've purchased with the Apple ID if you previously uninstalled or deleted it.

- Select the name of the app in the bottom-left area of the App Store on your Mac, or Sign In if you have not yet done so.
- After locating the purchased application that requires reinstallation, select the Download button.

INSTALL AND UNINSTALL APPLICATIONS FROM A DISC OR THE INTERNET ON A MAC

Applications can be downloaded and installed from a disc or the internet. You may uninstall an application if you no longer require it.

To install applications on your Mac, perform one of the following:

- To utilize internet-downloaded applications, double-click the disc image or package file (which resembles an open case) in the Downloads folder. Open the specified installer if it does not launch automatically, and then proceed with the on-screen prompts.
- Insert the disc containing the application onto the optical

drive of your Mac, or connect the disc to your Mac.

Uninstall Applications

Applications that were installed and downloaded from the web or a disc can be uninstalled.

- Select the Finder symbol in the Dock, followed by Apps in the Finder sidebar, on the computer.
- Perform one of the subsequent actions:
- ✓ Open the folder containing the application to search for the Uninstaller. Double-tap Uninstall [Application] or [Application] Uninstaller when prompted, and then adhere to the on-screen prompts.
- ✓ In the absence of a folder or uninstaller for an application: After the Dock, drag the application coming from the Applications location to the Trash.

Caution: The application will be deleted irreversibly from your Mac the following time you or the Finder delete it from the Trash. Files created with the application may no longer be accessible for reopening. When deciding whether to retain the application, retrieve it before removing it from the Trash. After locating the application in the Trash, select File > Reinstall.

Launchpad can be used to uninstall applications downloaded through the App Store.

DOCUMENT ACCESS ON A MAC

To launch a document on a Macintosh, perform a double-click operation on its icon located on the desktop.

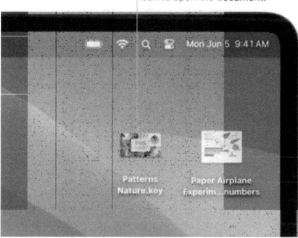

A desktop document in Numbers.

If a document's indicator is absent from the desktop, alternative methods exist for accessing the document on a Mac:

- Input the name of the desired document into the search field after selecting Spotlight from the menu bar; double-tap the document in the resulting list.
- Select the document from the Apple menu > Recent Items if you have recently worked on it.
- Launch the application associated with the document, select it from the Open dialogue (if present), or navigate to File > Open. You can select File > Open Recent in certain applications to access recently accessed documents.
- Select the Finder application from the Dock. Double-click the document's symbol or name after selecting Recents, iCloud Drive, Documents, or the folder containing the file from the Finder sidebar.

Before opening documents in iCloud Drive, the service must be configured.

UTILIZE MAC DESKTOP LAYERS

On a Mac, desktop stacks organize desktop files into organized groupings. An application automatically appends a file to the designated desktop layer upon saving.

A Mac desktop with four piles along the right margin of the screen, designated for documents, images, presentations, and spreadsheets.

Enable Desktop Stacking

- Select the desktop on your Mac, then select View > Use Stacks or type Control-Command-0. Additionally, you can control-click the desktop and select Use Stacks.

File Browsing Within A Desktop Stack

- Swipe the column to the left or right on your Mac using one finger on the Magic Mouse or two fingertips on the trackpad.

Collapse Or Expand A Desktop Stack

Perform one or more of the following on your Mac:

- To enlarge a collection, right-click on it from the desktop. To access an item when the stack is expanded, double-click it.
- To reduce the size of a collection, tap its down arrow symbol.

Modify The Grouping Of Desktop Stacks

Sorting piles by type (e.g., PDFs or images), date (e.g., the most recent opening or creation date of a file), or Finder annotations is possible.

- Select an option after clicking the desktop and selecting View > Group Stacks By on your Mac. Control-click the desktop and select Group Stacks By, followed by a desired option.

Alter The Visual Presentation Of Desktop Stacks

It is possible to adjust the size of icons, modify the inter-icon spacing, reposition symbol labels to the side, or display additional information (e.g., the number of files in a stack).

- Change the options by selecting View > Show View Options from the desktop menu on a Mac. Alternately, one may right-click the desktop, select Show View Options, and alter the settings.

ORGANIZE FILES IN FOLDERS

Including documents, images, music, and applications, everything on your Mac is organized in folders. To maintain organization as you establish documents, install applications, and perform other tasks, you can create new folders.

A window in Finder that displays files and folders. Highlighted in the shortcut menu is New Folder.

Establish A Folder

- Launch a Finder window on your Mac by clicking the Finder icon in the Dock; then, navigate to the location where you wish to construct the folder.

To establish the folder directly on the desktop, you may also select it by clicking the desktop icon.

- Select New Folder from the File menu, or hold Shift-Command-N.

When the New Folder option is obscured, it is not possible to construct a folder in the current directory.

- After entering the folder's name, select the Return key.

Transfer Objects To Folders

- Launch Finder by selecting the Finder icon from the Dock on your Mac.
- Perform one of the following:
- ✓ Drag an item into the folder to place it inside.
- ✓ Place several items in a folder: One of the selected products

should be dragged into the folder.

Each item that is selected is transferred to the folder.

✓ Place the contents of a window in a folder: After an icon appears to the left of the window title, position the cursor there and proceed to transfer the icon to the folder.

By simultaneously pressing and holding the Shift key while dragging the pointer through the title area, the icon will appear. Additionally, it is possible to navigate to the folder by dragging to the start of the window title, even before the icon appears.

Maintain a file in its initial location while assigning a duplicate to a folder: After selecting the item and holding down the Option key, drag the object into the folder.

✓ Maintain a file in its original spot while assigning it an alias in a new folder: To create an alias, hold down the Option as well as Command keys while dragging the item to the folder.
✓ Duplicate an item within its corresponding folder: Choose the item, then click Command-D or select File > Duplicate.
✓ Transferring files to an alternative hard drive: The files are dragged to the disc.
✓ Copy files to an alternative disc: While holding down the Command key, proceed to drag the files onto the disc.

Consolidate Multiple Objects Through A New Folder Rapidly
Creating a folder of items on the desktop or within a Finder window is a straightforward process.

- Choose all the items that you wish to group on the Mac.
- Control-click a selected item, and choose New Folder alongside Selection from the menu that appears.
- After entering the folder's name, select the Return key.

Merge Two Folders That Share The Same Name
It is possible to combine two folders bearing identical names that are situated in separate locations into a unified folder.

- While holding down the Option key on a Mac, drag a folder to the location where another folder with the same name is located. In the resulting dialogue, select Merge.

For the Merge option to be visible, a single folder must contain items that are absent from the other. When folders comprise distinct iterations of files with identical names, the sole available alternatives are Stop or Replace.

BACKUPS USING TIME MACHINE

One can utilize Time Machine to create backups of non-macOS installation-related files on a Mac, including documents, photographs, music, as well as applications. When Time Machine is activated, it executes hourly, daily, as well as weekly backups of your Mac's files automatically.

Local snapshots are also preserved by Time Machine, enabling the recovery of earlier versions of data even in the absence of an attached backup disc. Hourly images are generated and retained on the identical disc as the original data for 24 hours, or until disc space is depleted. The creation of local snapshots is limited to discs that utilize the Apple File System (APFS).

If you delete or modify a file by error, it is possible to reclaim it using Time Machine.

Click arrows to navigate
through backups.

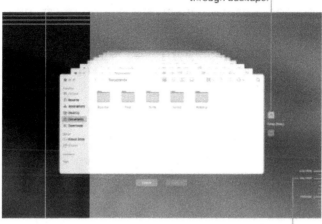

Backup timeline

The Time Machine window, which is comprised of nested Finder displays representing backups and features navigation indicators. The backup timeline and arrows on the right assist in navigating through backups to select which files to restore.

Even though Time Machine utilizes APFS to generate local snapshots on computers, it is advisable to backup your data to a location that isn't your internal disc. This could include a Time Capsule, an external hard disc, or a disc connected to your network. Thus, you will have the ability to restore your entire system to another Mac if your internal disc or Mac is damaged.

- Activate an external hard disc that you have connected to your Mac.

It is crucial to note that backups created on Macs running macOS 12 or later are only recoverable on Macs operating macOS 11 or later.

- Perform one of the subsequent actions:
- ✓ Configure a disc via the dialogue titled "Time Machine may back up your Mac": You are prompted to utilize the Time Machine backup disc to create a duplicate of your Mac if one is not already present. Select Setup from the Options menu that appears after hovering the mouse over the dialogue box, in order to utilize this disc as

a Time Machine backup. (Clicking Close will cause Time Machine to terminate and the disc to re-establish a normal connection.)

✓ In the Time Machine Settings, configure a disc: In the menu bar, select Launch Time Machine Settings by clicking the Time Machine icon.

Apple > System Settings should the Time Machine symbol not be visible in the menu bar. Down to "Time Machine," select "Show in Menu Bar" from the pulldown menu that appears after clicking Control Centre in the sidebar.

✓ By selecting the Add icon, you can insert a backup disc.

If one or more backup discs are already configured, that will determine which option appears.

Time Machine Backups Can Be Restored On A Mac

You can effortlessly retrieve misplaced items or previous versions of files from your Mac if you utilize Time Machine to create backups.

• Launch the corresponding application window on your Mac.

Launch the Documents folder, for instance, to retrieve a file that was deleted inadvertently.

There is no need to create a window if an element is absent from the desktop.

• In the Other folder, launch Time Machine using Launchpad. Although the Mac is connecting to the backup disc, a notification may appear.
• Navigate through local archives and backups by utilizing the arrows and timeline.

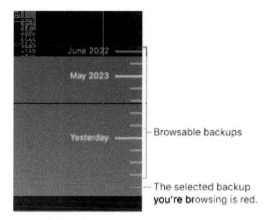

In the backup timeline, place checkboxes. As you navigate,
the backup is denoted by the red checkmark.

A backup that is in the process of loading or verifying on the backup disc is indicated by a checkmark that blinks from pale to semi-dark grey.

- After identifying several items (folders or the entire disc) that you wish to restore, choose Restore.

The original location of restored objects is reinstated. An instance of this would be the return of an item from the Documents folder to that location.

CHAPTER SIX

EDITING PHOTOS

Among other things, you can rapidly crop as well as rotate images, apply filters, and enhance photographs using the Picture editing tools. In order to test alterations, it is possible to duplicate photos as well as replicate modifications to other photos. You can reverse the modifications you've made to a photograph if you alter your mind.

MODIFY AN IMAGE OR VIDEO

- Perform the following actions within the Photos application on your Mac:
✓ Double-tap the thumbnail of an image or video, then select Edit from the toolbar.
✓ After selecting a thumbnail image or video, click Return.
- Perform one of the following:

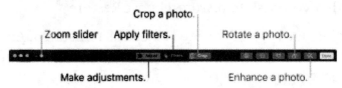

A Zoom slider and icons for adjusting, applying filters, cropping, rotating, and enhancing images are displayed in the Edit toolbar.

✓ To adjust the size of an image, simply click and drag the Zoom slider.
✓ Select the Adjust button to bring up the adjustment tools.
✓ Apply filters: To view filters that can be used to alter the appearance of a photo or video, select Filters.
✓ To display the available options for reducing a photo or video, select Crop.
✓ To counterclockwise rotate a photo or video, select the Rotate button from the toolbar. Click repeatedly until the desired orientation is achieved. By selecting the option and clicking the icon⟲, the image can be rotated clockwise.

✓ To instantly enhance a video or picture, select the Auto Enhance icon ✨ and the contrast and color of the image or video will be modified accordingly. Select Revert to Original or select Command-Z to undo the modifications.

· To cease modifying, select Return or select Done.

You may navigate to different elements by pressing the arrow keys while altering an image or video.

DUPLICATE AN IMAGE

To generate multiple iterations of a video or image, one must replicate it and modify the duplicate.

· On a Mac, launch the Photos application and choose the object to duplicate.
· Select Duplicate 1 Photo from the Image menu, or select Command-D.

To copy a Live Photo with the video portion included, select Duplicate; to duplicate the still picture only, select Duplicate as Still Picture.

Contrast Recordings Or Photographs Before And After Modification

It is possible to compare the modified version of an item to its original whilst modifying it.

· Double-tap an image or video to view it in the Photos application on your Mac, then select Edit from the toolbar.
· To view the original image, press and hold the M key or press down on the Without Adjustments icon.

Press and release the icon or the M key to view the modified item.

The Without Adjustments icon is located in the upper-left quadrant

of the window, adjacent to the window controls.

HOW TO COPY AND PASTE EDITED VIDEO OR IMAGE

Once you have completed editing a video or image, you can copy and transfer the modifications onto other files. Edits can be pasted simultaneously onto multiple objects.

Note: Settings from third-party extensions, the retouch tool, the red-eye tool, as well as the crop tool cannot be copied and pasted.

- Do so in the Photos application on your Mac by performing a double-click on an edited item, followed by selecting Edit from the toolbar.
- Select Image > Duplicate Edits.
- Control-click the item (or multiple items) to which you wish to apply the modifications.
- Navigate to Image > Paste Edits.

Additionally, in the editing view, you can Control-click an element and select Copy Edits or Paste Edits.

UNDO YOUR MODIFICATIONS

Rapid removal of modifications to an image or video is possible.

Perform any of the subsequent within the Photos application on your Mac:

- To undo the most recent modification, select Edit > Undo or enter Command-Z.
- To undo all modifications as well as restore the original image, click Image > Revert to Original after selecting the photo or video.

UTILIZE LIVE TEXT IN PHOTOS TO INTERACT WITH TEXT WITHIN AN IMAGE

Live Text allows you to duplicate and utilize the text that is displayed within an image. For instance, the text of a roadside sign could be copied and pasted into an email or text message.

An image of a real estate for sale sign featuring a menu containing the agent's phone number and Live Text capabilities (e.g., adding the number to Contacts, initiating a FaceTime call, sending a text message, and more).

- Launch a photograph containing text in the Photos application on your Mac.
- To select a section of text, hover the cursor over it and then drag it.
- Perform one of the following:
✓ To copy selected text, select Copy with a control-click or by pressing Command-C. The copied content can then be pasted into another application or document.
✓ To determine the meaning of a given text, control-click on it and select Look Up [text].
✓ To translate text, select Translate [text], control-click the selected text, and then select a language.

Please be advised that translation services may be limited in scope and unavailable in certain countries or regions.

✓ To locate the specified text on the web, control-click on it and select Search with [web search engine].

✓   To share a selection with others, control-click it, select Share, and then specify how you wish to distribute the text.

✓   Make contact via telephone: To initiate a FaceTime audio or video call, send a message to the specified number, or FaceTime video or audio call, choose the desired action with a control-click or the down arrow.

✓   Make contact via email: Choose the drop-down menu or control-click the selected item, and choose the option to compose an email or add the email address to Contact.

✓   Navigate to the following website: To view the website's information, control-click on it or select the down arrow, then access the URL in the browser or utilize Quick Look.

HOW TO USE QUICK NOTE

Regardless of your Mac activity, you can write down ideas as well as add connections using Quick Note. Maintaining the visibility of your Quick Note during its active state enables effortless selection and addition of data from other applications.

Commence a Quick Note

While engaged in another application and in need of jotting something down, a Quick Note can be conveniently initiated. Perform one of the subsequent actions:

- Utilize the shortcut symbol combination: hold down the Fn or Globe key, then select Q.
- Utilize hot corners: Select the note that appears after dragging the cursor to the lower-right corner of the display (the default hot corner for Quick Note). To modify or deactivate the hot corner.
- Utilize Safari to Import Safari content or Safari URLs into a Quick Note container.

Select the red Close icon located in the upper-left quadrant of a Quick Note to terminate it. To reopen the Quick Note, utilize one of the aforementioned methods.

To prevent the reopening of previously opened Quick Notes and instead initiate a new one, navigate to Notes > Settings and deselect "Always resume to last Quick Note."

Include Links To Safari In A Quick Note

- Launch Safari on your Mac and navigate to the site you wish to link to.
- Select Add to Quick Note or New Quick Note from the Share menu.

Upon revisiting the hyperlinked content on the webpage, a visual representation of the Quick Note shows up on the periphery of the screen as a visual reminder of the earlier entry.

Links to webpages as well as additional applications can also be added to Notes.

Safari Content Can Be Added To A Quick Note

It is possible to directly add highlighted text from a webpage to a Quick Note.

- Launch Safari on your Mac, navigate to the desired webpage, and then select the desired text to be added to a Quick Note.
- After selecting New Quick Note or Add to Quick Note via control-clicking the text.

The content of a link that displays in the Quick Note is highlighted in Safari. Upon subsequent visits to the webpage, the portion that has been highlighted remains in place.

Destroy the highlighted Safari connection from the Quick Note to eliminate it.

After a Brief Note

In the Notes application, your Quick Notes are located in the Quick Notes folder. They can be modified to include tables, keywords, and more. Consult one of the following:

- Enter a table

- Include keywords
- Include listings
- Include connections

It is not possible to secure a Quick Note.

APPLY CONTINUITY TO APPLE DEVICES TO COLLABORATE

You can utilize Continuity to sync your Mac with your other Apple devices, allowing you to work more efficiently and seamlessly transition between them.

A FaceTime-enabled iPhone is positioned adjacent to a Mac, where the connection is being transferred as denoted by the Handoff indicator located on the FaceTime application icon in the lower-right corner of the Dock.

Sign in to all of your devices with the same Apple ID to utilize Continuity features. Additionally, the gadgets must be equipped with Bluetooth® and Wi-Fi and satisfy system requirements. For a list of the system necessities for Continuity on Mac, iPhone, iPad, as well as Apple Watch, consult the Apple Support article.

AirDrop

AirDrop enables you to wirelessly and instantly share photos, videos, contacts, as well as anything else with those in your immediate vicinity. It simplifies the sharing process to an iPhone, iPad, iPod touch, or Mac employing dragging as well as dropping.

Airplay To Mac

Present, play, or share content from an additional Apple gadget on your Mac.

Approval and Auto-Unlock Via Apple Watch

Without entering a password, you can utilize your Apple Watch to access your Mac or authorize requests for authentication from your Mac.

The Continuity Camera

Utilize your iPhone to act as a webcam on your Mac, or capture an image or scan a document using an iPhone or iPad close to your Mac to have it display instantaneously.

Continuity Markup

Changes made to a PDF file or image edited on a Mac are immediately reflected on an adjacent iPhone or iPad, where they can be annotated and sketched upon employing Markup tools (or the Apple Pencil on the iPad).

Continuity Sketch

Utilizing a nearby iPhone or iPad, you can create a doodle that appears instantaneously on your Mac.

Handoff

Commence work on a message, email, or document on a single gadget and continue from where you've left off on another. Keynote, Mail, Safari, Maps, Messages, Reminders, Calendar, Contacts, Pages, as well as Numbers are all compatible with Handoff.

Instant Hotspot

Absence of Wi-Fi? Not a problem. Without requiring configuration, your Mac can establish an internet connection via the personal hotspot on the iPad or iPhone when the devices are nearby. Simply selecting the iPhone or iPad from the Wi-Fi menu on your Mac will activate your hotspot.

Phone Calls

Instead of using your iPhone to initiate or receive phone calls, utilize your Mac. Numerous applications, including FaceTime, Contacts, Safari, Mail, Maps, and Spotlight, can initiate phone calls. When you receive a phone call, a notification will appear. To respond, simply select the notification.

Sidecar

By utilizing your iPad as an additional display, you have the option of extending your workstation by displaying distinct applications and windows or displaying the same windows and applications as your Mac.

(SMS) Messages

MMS and SMS text messages can be sent and received directly from a Mac. You can reply to text messages from the nearest device, irrespective of the phone ownership of your contacts. Every message that is displayed on your iPhone is also displayed on your Mac.

Universal Clipboard

After copying and pasting text, images, photos, as well as videos from a single Apple gadget to another, the content is transferred. For instance, a recipe could be copied from Safari on a nearby iPhone and pasted into Notes on the same device.

Universal Control

When close to another Mac or iPad, you can collaborate across the devices using a single keyboard, trackpad, or connected mouse. Even content can be dragged between them; for instance, an Apple Pencil illustration on an iPad could be dragged to a Mac to be inserted into a Keynote presentation.

UTILIZE YOUR IPHONE AS A WEBCAM

By utilizing Continuity Camera, you can leverage the capabilities of your iPhone camera as well as additional video effects while using it as a webcam or microphone for your Mac. For a wired connection, you may utilize a USB cable or establish a wireless connection.

A MacBook Pro displaying a FaceTime session via an iPhone acting as a webcam.

Before Commencing,

Before utilizing the Continuity Camera function, the following must occur:

- Ensure that your Mac and iPhone are running macOS 13 or later as well as iOS 16 or later, respectively.
- For all Continuity Camera options to be accessible, macOS 14 must be installed on your Mac and iOS 17 must be installed on your iPhone.
- Authorize both devices using an identical Apple ID.
- Activate Bluetooth® and Wi-Fi on both devices.
- Ensure that your devices are compatible with the system.
- Attach a mount to your iPhone.

Employ the iPhone As A Microphone Or Webcam

- Launch any application that has camera or microphone access on your Mac, such as Photo Booth or FaceTime.
- In the settings or menu pane of the application, select the device you are using as the camera or the microphone.

Upon launching the Continuity application on the iPhone, audio or video can be streamed from the camera on the back to the Mac.

Note: For the iPhone to function as a microphone on a Mac without an integrated camera, the device must be in landscape orientation, stationary, and have the display turned off. Alternatively, you may use a USB cable to connect your iPhone to your Mac.

- Perform one of the following:
- ✓ To pause a video or audio on an iPhone, press Pause or slide up to activate the device.
- ✓ To re-establish the video or audio, select Resume on your iPhone, or select the Sleep/Wake button or side button to secure it.
- ✓ Discontinue employing the iPhone as a microphone or webcam: On a Mac, terminate the application.
- ✓ To deactivate the option to remove the device, press Disconnect on your device and then affirm that you wish to disconnect. The iPhone is deactivated from the microphone and camera lists within applications, as well as the sound input gadgets list in the Sound settings.

USB cable connection between your iPhone and Mac in order to re-insert it.

For optimal results, when charging your iPhone with the Continuity Camera enabled, utilize a USB cable.

Switch Automatically To the iPhone Camera

FaceTime as well as Photo Booth are two applications that can seamlessly transition to using the iPhone's camera interface on your Mac. For this to occur, your iPhone must:

- Concentrate on your Mac
- Turn off its displays
- Maintain a landscape-oriented
- Face you with its back camera or cameras facing away from obstructions.
- Avoid placing it in a pocket or on a desk flat.
- Maintain a stationary position

Previous usage of the iPhone as a webcam on a Mac may result in other Mac applications remembering it as the favored camera as well.

Establish the iPhone As The Default Microphone

You can configure your Mac to use the microphone on your iPhone by default.

- Select Apple > System Preferences on your Mac, then select Sound in the sidebar. (Depth may require the user to navigate.)
- Choose the iPhone from the list of devices that accept sound input.

On an iPhone, the Continuity application launches and begins capturing audio.

Activate The Desk View And Video Effects

When your iPhone is used as a webcam for a Mac, video conferencing capabilities can be accessed via the Video icon in the menu bar. One illustration of this is the workstation View, which presents a top-down perspective of the user's workstation, while Studio Light alters the background dimness while illuminating the face.

Should Your iPhone Not Appear As A Camera
Or Microphone Option, Then

Try the steps below if your iPhone is not visible in the camera or microphone inventory of an application or the Sound settings.

- Retest after connecting it to your Mac via a USB cable. (Detach and reconnect it if it is currently connected to a cable.)
- Please verify the following:
✓ You own an iPhone model XR or later.
✓ iPhone models running iOS 16 or later.
✓ Your Mac is running macOS 13 or a later version.
✓ The Continuity Camera is enabled in Settings > General > AirPlay & Handoff on your iPhone.

✓   The Mac is acknowledged by your iPhone as a trusted computer.

✓   Apple has enabled Wi-Fi, and Bluetooth, as well as a two-factor authorization on both the iPhone and Mac.

✓   Both your Mac and iPhone are authenticated with the same Apple ID. (This function is incompatible with Managed Apple IDs.)

✓   Both your Mac and iPhone are within 30 feet of one another.

✓   Neither your iPhone nor your Mac are broadcasting their cellular or internet connections.

✓   The selected video application has been updated to its most recent version.

USING DESK VIEW

You may utilize Desk View with FaceTime along with other applications to simultaneously display your face as well as an overhead view of your desk while using your iPhone as a webcam. There is no need for complicated configuration.

Desk View is exclusively accessible on iPhone 11 and later, excluding the iPhone SE.

Implement Desk View in FaceTime

- On a Mac, launch the FaceTime application.
- Using a stand accessory to connect your iPhone to your Mac, you can then utilize your iPhone as a webcam.
- Select the Desk View icon located in the upper-right quadrant of the video window after initiating the video call.

When Workstation View is activated, an overhead camera-like perspective of your workstation is displayed from above.

- To align the workstation with the camera, utilize the workstation View configuration interface. Drag the on-screen control located at the bottom of the window to adjust the magnification level. Click Share Workstation

View when you are prepared to share your workstation view during the video call.

- To disable Desk View, select Close Window from the Screen Share menu 🔲 in the upper-left corner of the Desk View window, or Desk View > Quit Desk View from the menu bar.

Employ Desk View In Conjunction With Other Applications
- On your Mac, launch a video capture application.
- Using a stand accessory to connect your iPhone to your Mac, you can then utilize your iPhone as a webcam.
- After selecting the Video option from the menu bar, select Desk View.

When Workstation View is activated, an overhead camera-like perspective of your workstation is displayed from above.

As an alternative, Desk View can be accessed via a Spotlight search.

- To align the workstation with the camera, utilize the workstation View configuration interface. Drag the on-screen control located at the bottom of the window to adjust the magnification level. When prepared, select the Start Desk View button.
- To share the contents of your workstation using a third-party application, select the workstation See the window for sharing via the application's sharing of screens function. Consult the developer's instructions or the application's menus as well as settings to discover how.
- To deactivate Desk View, select Quit Desk View from the menu bar or dismiss the Desk View window.

HOW TO USE AIRPLAY TO STREAM AUDIO AND VIDEO
- AirPlay enables you to transmit audio, videos, photos, and more wirelessly from your Mac to your preferred speakers (including the HomePod mini), Apple TV, and select smart TVs via a Wi-Fi connection. Simply connect all of your

gadgets, including your Mac, to the same Wi-Fi network.

A Macintosh computer along with compatible gadgets that support content streaming via AirPlay, such as a smart TV, HomePod compact speakers, and Apple TV.

Enjoy Music Through Your Preferred Speakers

- Stream music from your Mac to one or more HomePods or any other AirPlay 2-enabled speaker to achieve that large-band sound. Launch the Apple Music application on your Mac, navigate to the queued tracks, and then select a speaker by clicking the AirPlay audio symbol in the playback controls.

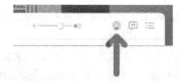

The application's playback controls (Music). The intensity control is positioned to the right of the AirPlay audio symbol.

While having dinner, expand your knowledge by listening to your preferred travel podcast.

Display Films And More On A Large Screen

Playing movies, television programs, as well as videos on the large display of your television is simple. Launch the program, select your Apple TV or smart TV, and then pick the AirPlay video symbol in the playback controls on the Mac.

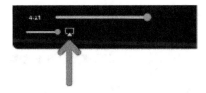

The controls for playback within the Apple TV application. The symbol for the AirPlay video is located beneath the progress indicator.

Recognized an outstanding online video that you would like to share with your friends? Utilize AirPlay directly within the Safari application.

Share Photographs With The Entire Room

AirPlay mirroring enables the Apple TV to display on-screen content from the Mac, such as a slideshow of wedding pictures curated in the Photos application, for all individuals in the room to see. Select Screen Mirroring from the Control Centre menu bar on your Mac, followed by the Apple TV or smart TV.

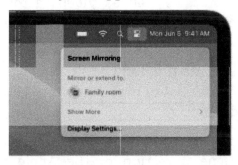

In the Control Centre, mirroring the screen options, which include Apple TV, are displayed.

By utilizing AirPlay on Mac, it is possible to stream video as well as listen to audio from an additional Apple gadget directly on your Mac.

CONTINUE FROM WHERE YOU LEFT OFF USING HANDOFF

Handoff enables the seamless continuation of an application initiated on a single Apple device (e.g., Mac, iPhone, iPad, or Apple Watch) on another device. For instance, you could begin replying to an email on your iPhone and complete it in Mail on your Mac. Handoff is compatible with a variety of Apple applications, including Safari, Calendar, Contacts, and Pages. Additionally, certain third-party applications might be compatible with Handoff.

The Handoff icon of an application from the iPhone Dock.

Your Apple devices must satisfy Continuity system requirements to utilize Handoff. Additionally, Wi-Fi, Bluetooth®, as well as Handoff must be enabled in the System Preferences of the Mac and the Settings of the iOS and iPadOS devices, respectively. On all of your gadgets, the same Apple ID must be used to log in.

When Handoff is enabled, you can manually copy and paste text, images, photos, as well as videos across gadgets using Universal Clipboard. Additionally, files can be copied between Mac computers.

Deactivate Or Activate Handoff
Note: Handoff functionality is not supported on devices that do not have a Handoff option.

- **With a Mac:** Select "AirDrop & Handoff" from the sidebar of the General section of the Apple menu > System Settings, then toggle "Allow Handoff between this Mac as well as your iCloud devices" to the active or inactive position. (Depth may require the user to navigate.)
- **When using an iPad, iPhone, or iPod touch:** Navigate to Settings > General > AirPlay & Handoff, here you can enable or disable Handoff.
- **On Apple Watch:** Navigate to My Watch > General in the Apple Watch app on your iPhone, then toggle Enable Handoff on or off.

Transferring Between Devices
- Moving from a Mac to an iPad or iOS device: On your iPad

or iPod touch (at the end of the Dock) or your iPhone (at the bottom of the app selector), the Handoff emblem of the application you are using on your Mac will appear. To continue using the application, tap.

- Connecting your Mac from an iOS or iPadOS device or Apple Watch: Depending on the Dock position, the Handoff icon of the application you are currently using on your iPhone, iPad, iPod touch, or Apple Watch will appear on your Mac near the right end of the Dock. Select the icon to proceed with your task within the application.

Additionally, you can rapidly transition to the application bearing the Handoff icon by pressing Command-Tab.

USING APPLE WATCH TO UNLOCK AND AUTHORIZE REQUESTS
Without entering a password, you can utilize your Apple Watch to access your Mac or authorize app requests when it is near your Mac while you are wearing it.

Note: To utilize these functionalities, you must ensure the following: You are utilizing an unlocked Apple Watch while your Mac is nearby; you are logged in with the identical Apple ID on both your Mac (model mid-2013 or later) and Apple Watch; and the use of two-factor authentication is enabled for your Apple ID.

Enable Approval And Auto-Unlock With Apple Watch
- In the sidebar that appears after selecting Apple > System Settings, pick Touch ID & Password. (Depth may require the user to navigate.)
- Select Apple Watch from the menu on the right, and then toggle the option next to your watch's name.

This option is accessible exclusively on Apple Watches equipped with watchOS 6 or later.

Unlock Your Mac
To rouse a dormant Mac, select any key from the keyboard or, in the case of a Mac laptop, launch the display. The screen displays the progress of unlocking your Mac.

Deny Application Proposals

Approval requests from your Mac are displayed on your Apple Watch when an application necessitates authorization on your Mac, such as to access notes or settings, examine passwords, or authorize application installations.

Apple Watch displaying a MacBook Pro's request for permission.

Tap the side button twice on the Apple Watch to grant permission for the requested task.

To determine whether your Mac is compatible with Auto Unlock and Approve with Apple Watch, navigate to Apple > About This Mac, select More Info, and then select System Report at the bottom of the screen. On the right, in the Network section of the sidebar, locate the phrase "Auto Unlock: Supported." Select Wi-Fi.

Logging in to the user account that is an admin on your Mac will allow you to enable Auto Unlock or Approve with Apple Watch for them, provided that their Apple ID employs two-factor authentication and their Apple Watch is equipped with the requisite version of watchOS.

CHAPTER SEVEN

ACCESSIBILITY

VISION-SPECIFIC ACCESSIBILITY FUNCTIONS

The accessibility functions in macOS facilitate the visibility of the displayed content. Additionally, your Mac can speak the contents of the display.

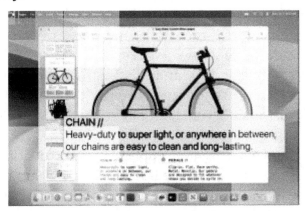

A Pages document in which the Hover Text window displays a large, high-resolution rendition of the document's text.

Voiceover Functionality

VoiceOver, the inbuilt screen reader that comes on your Mac, can be utilized to read aloud the text in Windows, documents, as well as webpages. You can operate your Mac using VoiceOver by employing the keyboard, trackpad motions, or a braille interface that can be refreshed. VoiceOver can be modified by utilizing VoiceOver Utility.

Zoom Capabilities

- Zoom in on the display to enlarge or magnify specific elements, thereby enhancing the legibility of the content. You can independently configure the magnification on a secondary display.
- Applying the Hover Text key will enlarge the current element beneath the cursor, including text, indicators, or

the user interface itself.
- To display a bigger version of the Touch Bar on the display of a Mac, enable Touch Bar magnification if the items in the Touch Bar are difficult to see.

Display Features
- Adjust the font size of text throughout multiple applications as well as system components using a single slider.
- Facilitate the process of locating the pointer on the display by altering its dimensions, and hue, or enlarging it upon rapid movement.
- Enhance legibility and distinguish between elements displayed on the screen through the implementation of color inversion, transparency reduction, color filtering, or tinting.
- When you activate applications, transition between workstations, view media featuring blinking or strobing lighting, or view rapidly animated images (such as GIFs), halt or reduce screen motion.

Please note that the "Dim flashing lights" feature is exclusive to Mac computers powered by Apple processors and supported media. Without exception, it is not recommended for the management of any medical ailment. Real-time processing of content occurs on the device.

Spoken Content Characteristics
Personalize the voice that your Mac uses to read aloud text and announcements, items that appear beneath the cursor, and anything else you type or select.

If available, listen to an overview of the visual content in films, television programs, and other media.

HEARING ACCESSIBILITY FEATURES IN MACOS
In addition to displaying and customizing captions on the screen, making and receiving Real-Time Text (RTT) communications, and

more, macOS includes accessibility features.

The Captions configuration dialogue. The user selects the custom design referred to as My Captions from the selection of styles for subtitles and captions. Placing itself to the right of the style name is an Edit icon.

Pair hearing devices designed for the iPhone with your Mac and modify their parameters using the Hearing Devices feature.

It should be noted that hearing devices designed specifically for iPhones are only compatible with specific Mac computers equipped with the M1 chip, while all Mac computers with the M2 chip can pair them.

Audio Attributes

One can enable screen flashing in response to alerts or announcements, as well as play stereo audio in mono mode. In addition to playing background audio, you can configure accessibility options for Apple earbuds as well as earbuds connected to your Mac. By utilizing an Apple-made Mac, one may configure Spatial Audio to track head movements while listening to Spatial Audio content.

RTT Attributes

Configure your Mac, if it supports it, to accept and send RTT communications.

Captions Capabilities

Make decisions regarding the formatting of subtitles and, if available, whether to use closed-captioning and SDH instead. Change Captions configurations for accessibility.

Live Captions Attributes

By leveraging the capabilities of the device's intelligence, your Mac can offer real-time captioning for audio, facilitating your comprehension of conversations, videos, and audio.

Please be advised that Live Captions (beta) is currently exclusive to Mac computers powered by Apple hardware and may not be accessible in all regions, countries, or languages. Live caption accuracy is subject to variation and should not be trusted during critical or life-threatening circumstances.

MOBILITY-ORIENTED ACCESSIBILITY FEATURES

macOS incorporates accessibility functionalities that enable users to interface with and navigate their Mac through the use of assistive devices, spoken commands, an onscreen keyboard, and other alternative methods of cursor control. Options can also be configured to facilitate the use of a trackpad or mouse.

The upper-left corner of the Mac desktop displays a numerical value next to each menu bar item. The Notes application is launched beneath the menu bar, with a numerical value displayed next to each option within the application.

Voice Control Functionality

- Voice Control enables users to interact with the content displayed on the screen, browse the desktop and applications, dictate and modify text, and perform additional tasks.
- In situations where the identification of a specific element or the need to manipulate a specific region of the display is unclear, it is possible to provide a numbered grid or designate onscreen components to facilitate item selection and screen navigation.
- While macOS includes an initial set of Voice Control commands, users can develop their commands and employ a customized vocabulary.

Keyboard Characteristics

- By enabling Full Keyboard Access, you can utilize the Tab key and other keys to navigate through all user interface elements on your Mac, as opposed to relying on the mouse or trackpad.
- The implementation of Sticky Keys and Slow Keys facilitates key pressing on a physical keyboard.
- By enabling the Accessibility Keyboard, users can operate their Mac using an onscreen keyboard instead of relying on a physical keyboard. You can personalize the navigation features and advanced typing (including typing suggestions) to access your preferred applications.
- By activating Dwell with the Accessibility Keyboard, mouse movements can be executed using head or eye-tracking technology.

Pointer Control Functionalities

- Configure preferences to facilitate mouse and trackpad use. For instance, modify the response time of the trackpad or mouse when an item is double-clicked. Or utilize the three-finger drag, with or without the drag lock.

Alternate pointer actions enable the execution of mouse operations (e.g., left-clicking or dragging and dropping) through the utilization of keyboard shortcuts, assistive switches, or facial expressions (e.g., smiling or opening the mouth). Revise the Pointer Control configurations to improve accessibility.

- Mouse Keys enable the user to manipulate the pointer and execute mouse commands by utilizing either a numeric keypad or the keyboard.
- Utilize a head pointer to manipulate the pointer in response to facial or head movements detected by the built-in or connected camera on your Mac.

Switch Control

Switch Control enables you to control your Mac, input text, and interact with on-screen elements using one or more adaptive accessories. Switch Control navigates a user interface or panel until an item is selected or an action is executed via a switch. See Control Switch Usage.

SPEECH ACCESSIBILITY FEATURES IN MACOS

macOS incorporates accessibility improvements such as voice-over functionality and the ability to generate a synthesized voice that closely resembles the user's own.

Live Speech

Using synthesized speech in-person conversations or applications such as FaceTime, you may hear what you compose spoken aloud if you are mute or have lost your words over time.

Individual Voice

Individuals who are at risk of verbal impairment have the option to generate a synthesized voice that closely resembles their own.

Please note that Personal Voice is restricted to Mac computers powered by Apple silicon and is not offered in every language.

Personal Voice is exclusive to Live Speech and third-party applications, including Augmentative as well as Alternative Communication (AAC) applications, that you grant permission for their use. Utilize Personal Voice exclusively to generate a device voice that closely resembles your own, and solely for personal, non-commercial purposes.

GENERAL ACCESSIBILITY FUNCTIONS

macOS contains accessibility functions that simplify the process of activating and deactivating various accessibility features and inputting Siri commands.

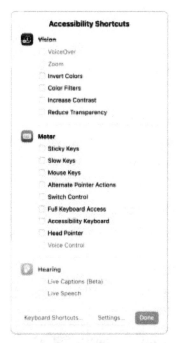

The Accessibility Shortcuts panel enumerates features that pertain to the senses of sight (e.g., color filters), motor function (complete keyboard access), and hearing (live captions (beta)).

Siri

Conversely, type your Siri commands rather than saying them aloud.

Shortcut

Make rapid changes to the state of different accessibility features by utilizing Accessibility Shortcuts.

OBTAIN A BLUETOOTH CONNECTION

Link an additional audio device, such as a headphone, keyboard, mouse, or trackpad, to your Mac via Bluetooth®.

Establish A Bluetooth Connection

- Ensure that the device is powered on and discoverable; for specifics, consult the device's documentation.
- From the Apple menu > System Preferences on your Mac, select Bluetooth in the sidebar. (Depth may require the user to navigate.)
- Click Connect while hovering the pointer over the gadget in the list.

When prompted, select Accept (or input a sequence of digits followed by input).

Additionally, by selecting the device from the menu bar and tapping the Bluetooth status icon, you may link the gadget via Bluetooth to your Mac. You can include the symbol in the menu bar via Control Centre settings if it is not already present.

Detach The Bluetooth Accessory

- Navigate to Apple > System Preferences on your Mac, then select Bluetooth in the sidebar. (Depth may require the user to navigate.)
- Press the Disconnect button while hovering the pointer over the gadget in the list.

To prevent an automatic reconnect of a device, select it via Control-click and then Forget. Re-establishing the connection is necessary in order to utilize it at a later time.

HOW TO USE AIRPODS ON MAC

Upon proximity and readiness for use with a Mac, AirPods can be employed for music listening, Siri functionality, and phone call management.

Connect The Airpods To The Mac.

- Lift the cover of the case containing the AirPods.
- Until the indicator light illuminates white, hold down a combination of the buttons for setting up on the rear of the case or the volume control switch (on AirPods Max only).
- Navigate to Apple > System Preferences on your Mac, then select Bluetooth in the sidebar. (Depth may require the user to navigate.)

Using the Control Centre settings, you can add the Bluetooth status symbol or Sound control to the bar's menu to facilitate the connection of your AirPods.

- Select Connect after hovering the pointer across your AirPods in the listing of gadgets on the right.

You have the option of configuring AirPods to link to your Mac immediately or only when they were last connected.

Modify Airpods Configuration On A Mac
- Ensure that your AirPods have been linked to your Mac while wearing them.
- Navigate to Apple > System Preferences on your Mac, then select the AirPods' name in the sidebar. (Depth may require the user to navigate.)
- Modify the AirPods' control schemes. (Options differ between models.)

Conserve Power On Your Mac
Your Mac is pre-configured to be energy efficient, with Compressed Memory as well as Application Nap functioning to maintain speed and conserve power. Nonetheless, energy consumption can be further optimized in many ways.

It should be noted that the availability of certain options might differ based on the Mac.

Sleep Your Mac System.
Your Mac remains powered on while in slumber mode, but

it utilizes significantly less energy. Additionally, a Mac can be awoken from slumber in less time than it takes to boot.

- Select Sleep from the Apple menu on the computer.

Optimally utilize your battery

Adjusting the following settings on a Mac laptop can help you maximize the battery's life while lowering energy consumption.

- Navigate to Apple > System Preferences on your Mac, then select Battery in the sidebar. (Depth may require the user to navigate.)
- Select one of the following options from the pop-up menu located to the right of Low Power Mode: • Always, Only on Battery, or Only on Power Adapter.
- ✓ Enable Optimized Battery Charging as well as "Manage battery longevity" by selecting the Info icon adjacent to Battery Health on the right.
- ✓ Enable "Automatic graphics swapping" and "Put hard discs to sleep when possible" by selecting Options from the menu on the right.

Deactivate Your Display When Inactive

- Select System Preferences from the Apple menu, followed by Lock Screen in the sidebar. (You may have to scroll down).
- Carry out one of the subsequent actions:
- ✓ Tap the pop-up menu to the right of "Deactivate battery power on the screen when not in use," then select an option.
- ✓ Select an option from the pop-up menu that appears to the right of "Pulse off display on power adapter when inactive."

Reduce The Display's Brightness

Attenuate the display to its minimum level of comfort. As an illustration, the luminance of the display may be comparatively lower in a dimly lit room as opposed to direct sunlight.

- Utilize the Displays settings or the luminance controls on your keyboard to reduce the screen's luminosity.

You can also configure the display of your Mac laptop to automatically dim when it is powered by battery life.

Turn Bluetooth And Wi-Fi Off

If Bluetooth® and Wi-Fi are not required, disable them. Energy is consumed regardless of whether they are not in use.

- *Disconnect Bluetooth:* Select Apple > System Preferences on your Mac, and then tap Bluetooth in the sidebar. (Depth may require the user to navigate.) Disable Bluetooth on the right side.
- Disable Wi-Fi by navigating to Apple > System Preferences > Network in the sidebar of your Mac. (Depth may require the user to navigate.) Disable Wi-Fi by selecting it from the list of devices on the right.

Disconnect Devices And Terminate Applications

- **Accessories:** Disconnect any unused accessories from the device, including external hard drives.
- **Linked external drives:** Disconnect an external drive from your Mac if using one, including an Apple USB SuperDrive.
- **Applications:** Uninstall applications that are not in use. Even a dormant application may be active in the background, ingesting unnecessary power.

Make Alternative Energy-Saving Selections

Select options within the Battery or Energy Saver settings that facilitate energy conservation. Permitting other computers access to shared resources on a sleeping Mac, such as music playlists or printers, could potentially increase the frequency at which the Mac enters sleep mode.

Select Apple > System Settings on your Mac, and then perform one of the subsequent actions:

- From a Mac laptop, select the Battery option from the sidebar. (Depth may require the user to navigate.)

- In the sidebar of a Mac desktop computer, select the Energy Saver option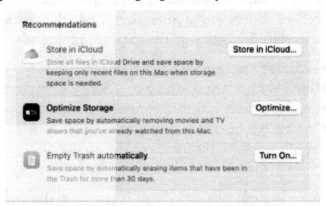. (Depth may require the user to navigate.)

HOW TO OPTIMIZE MAC'S STORAGE CAPACITY

MacOS can assist in freeing up space on a computer by optimizing its storage space. For instance, you can store files, photographs, videos, Apple TV movies as well and programs, as well as email attachments in iCloud while space is limited, thereby making them accessible on demand. The storage capacity of files on a Mac is not occupied, and the original files can be downloaded whenever necessary. Optimised versions of your pictures as well as recent files are consistently present on your Mac.

For guidance on optimizing storage space through the deletion of unnecessary files."

- Navigate to Apple > System Preferences on your Mac, then select General in the sidebar. (Depth may require the user to navigate.)
- Navigate to the Storage option on the right.
- Examine the suggestions and decide regarding the optimization of storage space on your Mac.

Recommendations

Store in iCloud	Store all files in iCloud Drive and save space by keeping only recent files on this Mac when storage space is needed.	Store in iCloud...
Optimize Storage	Save space by automatically removing movies and TV shows that you've already watched from this Mac.	Optimize...
Empty Trash automatically	Save space by automatically erasing items that have been in the Trash for more than 30 days.	Turn On...

Recommendation	Description
Maintain in iCloud	When space is at a premium on your Mac, store files from the

	Desktop as well as Documents folders in iCloud Drive, pictures and videos in iCloud Photos, messages as well as attachments in iCloud, and only recently viewed files in iCloud Pictures to optimize storage. Subsequently, in the iCloud window of Apple ID settings, Pictures settings, as well as Messages settings, it is possible to modify these configurations
Streamline Storage	While storage capacity is limited, conserve data by performing the following: automatically delete Apple TV movies and TV programs that have already been viewed; and retain only recent email attachments upon this Mac.
Trash is automatically emptied	Delete items from the Trash immediately if they have been there for over 30 days. This configuration is subsequently modifiable within the Finder.

macOS clears secure caches as well as logs when space is limited on a Mac. These logs and caches contain transient database documents, delayed downloads, staged macOS as well as application updates, Safari website data, as well as more.

It should be noted that recommendations solely pertain to the partition housing the home directory if the disc is partitioned.

MANAGING HOME ACCESSORIES
Five categories of accessories that you add to Home are displayed

at the highest point of the Home screen:

- Climate
- Light
- Security
- Speakers and Televisions

Individually enumerated accessories are also present in other sections, such as the chambers that have been added, beneath the categories.

Select Explore in the sidebar to view an introduction and suggestions for utilizing compatible smart home gadgets with the Home application.

Accessory categories

Click an accessory
to control it.

Control an accessory by clicking its icon in the tile of the Home application on your Mac to toggle it on or off. To access the accessory's controls, click its name in the tile.

The set of controls that are accessible is accessory-specific. For instance, certain lightbulbs permit the modification of luminance or color. Streaming devices and set-top boxes may only feature an

Activate switch.

To see every accessory in a category as well as their respective uses, select a category from the menu that appears at the highest point of the Mac application.

Command An Accessory Using A Variety Of Functions
Multiple functional accessories are governed by a single accessory tile. For instance, in the case of a ceiling fan featuring an integrated light, both the fan speed and light intensity can be managed through a single tile. At the highest point of the display, accessory categories are used to combine sensors.

The set of controls that are accessible is accessory-specific.

- Within the Home application on your Mac, select the tile representing a multifunctional accessory.
- To observe or control a feature, select it by clicking on it.

Place An Accessory In A Different Room
An accessory can be transferred from one room to another or added to another.

- In the sidebar of the Home application on your Mac, select Home or a Room.
- Position the accessory tile in the periphery to occupy a room.

To modify the appearance of an accessory tile in Home, utilize the control-click function.

Alter the designation of an accessory
- In the sidebar of the Home application on your Mac, select Home.
- Navigate to the bottom-right corner of the tile and select the Options icon next to the accessory's name.
- Enter a new name for the accessory after removing the old one, and then select the Close icon in the upper-right corner.

CHAPTER EIGHT

ENSURING CONFIDENTIALITY

Privacy is a significant consideration when utilizing applications that transmit data over the internet. macOS incorporates security functionalities that serve to fortify user privacy and regulate the extent to which personal and Mac-related data is disclosed online.

USING SCREEN TIME

You may track your children's computer use and restrict their respective positions' access to websites using Screen Time.

Select System Preferences from the Apple menu, then Screen Time in the sidebar. (Depth may require the user to navigate.)

USING PRIVACY SETTINGS IN SAFARI

Safari provides a multitude of functionalities that enable users to manage their online privacy. By utilizing private browsing, Safari will not log the websites you visit or the files you download. A Privacy Report details which users have been prevented from following you. In addition to enabling or disabling pop-up windows, you can delete cookies from your Mac.

MANAGING THE PERSONAL DATA

Web browsers and other applications can collect and utilize location-based data using Location Services. You have the option of entirely disabling Location Services or specifying which applications are permitted to access your location data.

Certain applications may access and utilize data from your calendar, contacts, photographs, or reminders. Some applications may request access to your Mac's microphone or camera.

Review the subsequent subjects:

- Permit applications to track the placement of your Mac.
- Manage access to your photographs
- Manage the accessibility of your contacts

- Manage access to your calendars
- Regulate who can access the camera
- Manage Macintosh microphone access

DETERMINE WHETHER OR NOT TO SHARE ANALYTICS DATA

Your assistance would enable Apple to enhance the efficacy and quality of the goods and services it provides. macOS is capable of autonomously gathering analytics data from your Mac and transmitting it to Apple for examination. The information is submitted to Apple anonymously and only with your consent.

To determine whether analytics data is transmitted to Apple, access the Privacy & Security interface.

After selecting Apple > System Settings, proceed to the Privacy & Security section by selecting Analytics & Improvements🖐 from the sidebar. (Depth may require the user to navigate.)

ESTABLISH A FIREWALL

You can safeguard your privacy with a firewall by preventing your Mac from engaging in unauthorized network communications. You may additionally utilize "stealth mode," which prevents unauthorized access to your Mac via the web, with the firewall enabled.

To configure and personalize your firewall, navigate to Network settings.

Select Apple > System Preferences, followed by a click Firewall on the right after selecting Network in the sidebar. (Depth may require the user to navigate.)

CONFIGURE YOUR MAC FOR SECURITY

Here are some measures that can be taken to increase the security of your Mac.

Employ Strong Passwords

In order to safeguard your information, it is advisable to implement password protection on your Mac. Select passwords that are not readily surmised.

Establish Passkeys

By using a passkey, it is possible to access an app or website account without having to generate and retain a password. Instead of a password, passkeys authenticate users via Touch ID or Face ID.

Demand That Users Check In

If unauthorized individuals obtain physical access to your Mac, you must create unique user accounts for each user and mandate that they log in. This feature hinders unauthorized access to the Mac. Additionally, it implements a security mechanism that restricts access to individual user files and settings. Users are unable to modify or access the settings or files of other users.

While Your Mac Is Dormant, Safeguard It

It is possible to configure the Mac to log out the current user after a specified period of inactivity Additionally, a password should be necessary to activate the device from hibernation or the screen saver.

Restrict The Quantity Of Administrative Users

A Mac may be granted administrator privileges to one or more users. The administrator is the individual who initially configures the Mac by default.

Administrators can modify settings, install and uninstall software, and create, manage, and eliminate users. An administrator should therefore establish a standard user account for situations in which administrator privileges are unnecessary. The potential damage is considerably reduced when the security of a standard user has been compromised as opposed to when the user possesses administrator privileges. When your Mac is shared by multiple users, restrict the number of individuals granted administrator privileges.

FileVault Safeguarded The Data That Was Encrypted On Your Mac

The data of users possessing a Mac equipped with Apple silicon or an Apple T2 Security Chip is automatically encrypted. FileVault enhances security measures by mandating the use of a login password to access one's data.

USING PASSKEY TO ACCESS AN ACCOUNT

By using a passkey, it is possible to access an app or website account without having to generate and retain a password. Instead of a password, passkeys authenticate users via Touch ID or Face ID.

Touch ID can be utilized to sign in if configured on a Mac or Magic Keyboard. Alternatively, you can use Face ID to authenticate and sign in with an iPad or iPhone by scanning a QR code.

Establish A Passphrase For A New Account

When creating a new account, you must input your account name and then select "Submit."

To generate a passkey, iCloud Keychain needs to be configured on a Mac.

When the option for saving a passkey for the user account appears, select the desired method of authentication:

- ✓ To activate Touch ID on your computer, touch the Touch ID sensor with your finger.
- ✓ Decode a QR code using an iPad or iPhone: Proceed to Other Options.
- ✓ Key for external security: Select Other Options.

Substitute A Passkey For The Current Account's Password

- Enter your password to access the account.
- Select System Preferences from the Apple menu, then select Passwords in the sidebar. (Depth may require the user to navigate.)
- To access the website's information, click the Info icon.
- Select Password Change on the Website.

Access An Account By Entering A Passkey

- Enter your account name and then select the account

name field on the account sign-in page.

- Select your account from the enumerated recommendations.
- Perform one of the subsequent actions:
- ✓ Touch ID users on Macs are instructed to place their finger on the Touch ID sensor.
- ✓ **Should you own an iPad or iPhone:** After selecting Other Options and "Passkey from a nearby device," proceed to scan the QR code.

  Bluetooth® must be enabled in the Settings > Bluetooth menu on an iOS device. Additionally, Bluetooth must be enabled on the Mac.
- ✓ **Key for external security:** After selecting Other Options and selecting "Security key," proceed with the on-screen instructions.

HOW TO PROTECT YOUR APPLE ID

Apple services such as the App Store, Apple Music, iCloud, iMessage, and FaceTime are accessible via your Apple ID. The email address and password used to access your account, along with the contact, payment, and security information utilized across various Apple services, are all components of your account.

Guidelines For Optimizing The Security Of An Apple ID

- Your Apple ID should not be shared with anyone, not even family members.

Up to five trusted individuals can be designated as Account Recovery Contacts to assist with account restoration in the event of a lockout. Additionally, a person can be designated as a Legacy Contact in your will.

Family Sharing enables the sharing of purchases, subscriptions, a family calendar, and other items without the need to share Apple IDs.

- Your password, security inquiries, verification code, recovery key, and any other account security information should not be shared with a third party. Apple will never request this information from you.

- Avoid reusing the password for your Apple ID on other online accounts.
- Always log out at the end of your session when using a public computer to prevent unauthorized access to your account.
- Enable two-factor authentication for account security. When you generate a fresh Apple ID on a device running iOS 13.4, iPadOS 13.4, macOS 10.15.4, or a later version, two-factor authentication is implemented automatically on your account. Enable two-factor authentication if you previously managed to create an Apple ID account without it.

Commence Using Mac Accessibility Features

The accessibility features of macOS can assist with speech, vision, hearing, and physical motor activities, among other things. You have the option to enable accessibility features in the Accessibility settings at any time, even if you did not do so during Mac setup.

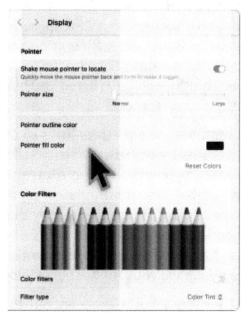

**Facility Accessibility Preferences for displaying a sizable
pointer with a personalized outline color.**

- Select Apple > System Preferences on your Mac, then select Accessibility in the sidebar. (Depth may require the user to navigate.)

Right-hand in the Accessibility settings are five main categories of features:

✓ **Vision:** Employ these functionalities to enlarge text or the pointer, decrease on-screen motion, and perform additional actions. Or, have the Mac display the content of the screen.

✓ **Hearing:** Operate your Mac with Made for iPhone hearing devices by utilizing these functionalities, which also enable you to display and modify captions on the screen, engage in Real-Time Text (RTT) calls, obtain Live Captions of audio, as well as more.

It should be noted that hearing devices designed specifically for iPhones are only compatible with specific Mac computers equipped with the M1 chip, while all Mac computers using the M2 chip can pair them, Live Captions (beta) is not accessible in all regions, countries, or languages. Live caption accuracy is subject to variation as well as should not be trusted during critical or life-threatening circumstances.

✓ **Motor:** Employ these functionalities to regulate your Mac and applications by utilizing assistive technology, spoken instructions, keyboard keys, on-screen keys, or other alternative methods to manipulate the pointer. Additional configurations can be made to simplify the operation of the trackpad and mouse.

✓ Use these functions to generate a synthesized voice that tunes like you, have your input spoken aloud, and more.

Please note that Personal Voice is restricted to Mac computers powered by Apple silicon as well as is not offered in every language. Personal Voice is exclusive to Live Speech as well as third-party applications, including Augmentative as well as Alternative Communication (AAC) applications, that you grant permission for their use. Utilize Personal Voice exclusively to generate a device voice that closely resembles your own, and solely for personal, non-commercial purposes.

✓   In general, utilize these functionalities to input Siri requests and toggle accessibility characteristics on or off with the aid of Accessibility Shortcuts.

www.ingramcontent.com/pod-product-compliance
Lightning Source LLC
LaVergne TN
LVHW051654050326
832903LV00032B/3804